JOHN TANTALON

The Haunted Realms of Surrey and Hampshire

First edition

This book was professionally typeset on Reedsy.
Find out more at reedsy.com

For Mary Rye Scott
1936-2023

Contents

Foreword

I first encountered The Haunted Realms of Surrey and Hampshire in early 2007. With family living there, it was the perfect venture to begin a journey to discover its ghosts. During a trip to The Isle of Wight, I discovered the rich tapestry of supernatural tales of the Island. The many books by author Gay Baldwin and impressive ghost walks, courtesy of Marc Tuckey and Ghost Island, hooked me. The many ghostly stories and legends paved the way for many years of interest in the area and, eventually, the book you are now reading.

This book's chapters result from fifteen years of thorough research, interviews, and direct observation. I was fortunate to interview many people from stately homes, pubs, restaurants, shops, and castles. With only one exception (I shall not divulge details), I was met with exceptional hospitality along the way. The people who have rallied witnesses from near and afar. Those who travelled on days off for interviews and even stayed awake to relay ghostly tales after finishing a night shift.

The contents of this book, although detailed, are not exhausted. There is enough material about Surrey and Hampshire to release a second book (and a separate book on The Isle of Wight). So please keep your eyes peeled for a potential future book on the other ghosts of Surrey and Hampshire.

Please sit back and get comfortable. Pour yourself a drink and dim the lights if you dare. Prepare to enter.

The Haunted Realms of Surrey and Hampshire

Acknowledgement

The Haunted Realms of Surrey and Hampshire has been a roller coaster ride of supernatural shenanigans from start to finish. I would like to thank everybody who helped me along the way.

The excellent staff and customers of The Star Inn, Godalming. Andy, Stu and everybody else, I owe you all a pint.

Louise and all the brilliant staff from Hartsfield Manor. It speaks volumes when people will wait after finishing a nightshift to relay their thoroughly ghostly tales.

Russ and the staff and customers from The Royal Oak, Guildford. One seriously haunted pub.

Amanda, the kind lady who relayed the stories to me of the Guildford woods.

Dan Hill, "Cheers mate".

The amazing staff of The Star Inn, Bentley (I interviewed four different pubs called The Star, one with a cursed skull in its basement)

Mark Tuckey and Ghost Island walks. Without a doubt the catalyst for this book.

Gay Baldwin. Thank you so much for your incredible books on the most haunted island in the world.

There are many, many, many more people to thank. you all know who you are.

Cover design created once again by the great Rob Warden.

Back cover photo by Jonathan Ley (hope to see you on the next ghost walk)

And you, the reader for buying this book.

Aldershot

The Hampshire town of Aldershot sits thirty-one miles southwest of London. Records dating back to The Domesday Book of 1086 refer to the location. The name may have derived from alder trees found in the area (from the Old English' alder-holt' meaning copse of alder trees).

In 1854, during the Crimean War, Aldershot Garrison was established as the first permanent training camp for the British Army. In 1914 Aldershot had the largest army camp in the country, with twenty percent of the British Army being based in and around the town. Aldershot has since held the title Home of the British Army ever since.

With several highly decorated residents past and present and countless tales of victorious battles, Aldershot has a story or two to tell. It also has its fair share of ghost stories. The town and its illustrious military past most certainly yield an impressive history.

I first travelled to Aldershot in early 2007. Not far from the address I stayed at is the oldest church in Aldershot. The Church of St Michael the Archangel is the parish church for the town and dates to the 12th century. There was almost certainly an earlier church on the site. Not far from the church is a property with an incredible connecting story. I have enjoyed many happy years visiting the area and discovering its many ghostly tales.

The House of Old Mother Squalls

At the bottom of the long and steep Eggars Hill sits Weybourne Road. Beyond a railway bridge and on the border of Surrey sits a charming and weathered house. The building is the previous site of the ancient Fox and Hounds Inn. Now a residential property, the house has a reputation for strange occurrences over the years. Some locals refer to the location as 'The House of Old Mother Squalls'

According to local records, a woman lived here in 1640. She was considered by many to be a witch. Stories abounded of unholy activity carried out within the building. On more than one occasion Old Mother Squalls had provided evidence of a supernatural nature to anybody foolish enough to cross her. A story existed that the woman maintained the ability to main or plate a horse's tail instantly and curl. She could twist a cow's tail just as quickly and terrify a dog or cat so the animals would flee with their tales between their legs.

The woman who gave birth was Nell Gwynne, and the child's father was Charles II, but the illegitimate boy was born dead. It was a secret birth that could have changed the course of history and been the cause of anyone who was concerned with the affair losing their heads. In February 1678, she was hastily summoned to attend confinement in the dead of night.

There has always been a persistent rumour that the Parish Church of Aldershot received a grant from Charles II. Legend states that the gift would continue if the yew tree flourished, but alas, the church records reveal no such transaction. In the dark silence of the early morning, unknown individuals buried a little box under the yew tree inside the church gate, the village priest having been aroused from his bed to perform the required ceremony.

The sound of unexplained, unnatural footsteps along the path has been reported. Accounts exist from residents who claim to have heard strange shuffling noises in the confines of the church grounds. Tapping sounds akin to an older woman with a stick rattling the church window close to the famous yew tree are also documented. There have been few such reports since 1971-76.

I have spent much time on the grounds of The Church of St Michael the Archangel. The ancient gravestones remain preserved throughout the peaceful church grounds. I have attempted to contact staff from the church to ascertain the precise location of the legendary yew tree. Unfortunately, I have had no reply on the matter to date.

The front entrance of the church

In Aldershot, the city centre is Wellington Road. Directly from the Naafi Roundabout is a steep road called Gun Hill. At the top of the hill amongst shady trees and fences is the ominous and imposing sight of the Cambridge Military Hospital. Constructed in 1879, the hospital would serve the various military camps of the town. After World War Two, the public also used the hospital until its closure in 1996. It would seem, however, that the hospital is not entirely vacant.

The frightening tale of a ghostly grey lady has existed for many years. It is stated that the legend of the Grey Lady stems from a sister in the Queen Alexandra Imperial Nursing Service. She inadvertently administered a fatal dose to a patient and, in her remorse, afterwards committed suicide by throwing herself over the hospital balcony.

The Grey Lady is said to have been seen and heard by patients and staff at the century-old hospital many times, apparently making her rounds as she often did during her lifetime. Her last recorded appearance was in 1969 when a night watchman saw her. The ghost appears when the staff are under pressure, hectic perhaps, or understaffed; a spirit that attempts to be benign and comforting but can be very frightening for those who encounter it.

Ward 13 used to have a balcony, but the original hospital has been built around it, and various floors and corridors have been added. However, it is still most frequently in the vicinity of the ominously numbered Ward 13 that the ghostly Grey Lady walks.

The location has now been converted to housing and renamed Gun Hill Park. Much of the area is now completely redeveloped and unrecognisable, yet the main building remains. The new tenants who occupy this legendary location enjoy an impressive view over Hampshire and Surrey from the one-time hospital tower. Does the Grey Lady stand beside them?

A recent image of the hospital

On the Aldershot's border and the outskirts of Surrey and Hampshire is an area with a haunted reputation. Alma Lane is a steep stretch of road which, on record, has existed since before1815. At this same time, a military runner would travel the extensive route to deliver a message to the military in Aldershot. The news of Wellington's success at Waterloo was tragically cut short when bandits brutally murdered the runner. It is said that the tragic messenger continues to traverse the site of Alma Lane, still attempting to relay news of the victory.

Fellow travellers can hear his heavy boots pounding the road on winter nights. Alma Lane is now entirely a residential area, but the path and legend of the tragic messenger remain. The sound of ghostly footsteps has been observed sitting somewhere between Beam Hollow and The Alma public house. However, it has been many years since anybody encountered the messenger's tragic spirit.

Ghostly footsteps walk along Alma Lane

Of all the fantastic tales of Aldershot, none can compare to the following terrifying story.

It was a pleasant, warm summer evening, 12th August 1983. A local man named Alfred Burtoo fished on the bank of the Basingstoke Canal. The evening was calm and the water still as he sat there waiting for the first catch of the night.

Alfred poured himself a cup of tea from his flask and lit a cigarette. It was going to be a long evening. The 77-year-old Mr Burtoo was a regular to the area and had fished the waters for many years. The banks, although treacherous in places, were stable; there had been no severe rainfall for quite some time. The sound of the nearby army barracks clock informed him that it was now one o'clock in the morning. Fifteen minutes later, he would notice something strange.

Alfred became aware of movement from his side. His dog Tiny stood up from the bank and looked towards nearby trees. The dog growled nervously. Suddenly, a bright light appeared from the direction of the trees. The glow, accompanied by movement from its vicinity, showed something was approaching.

Apart from seeing a policeman on military patrol, Alfred had not seen anybody that night until now. Two figures of about four feet in height walked towards the startled man. They wore green overalls which appeared sculpted to their bodies. They wore helmets with black visors. Alfred had spent time in the military and, when interviewed, stated that he was in no way afraid of the two figures. If anything, he was thoroughly intrigued.

The figures motioned Alfred to walk with them towards the light. He obliged and soon found himself walking along a narrow towpath. At the end of the path stood a craft, metallic and around forty feet in size. The figures motioned him to some steps he would ascend and then find himself within an octangular-shaped room. Even then, Burtoo maintained, "I wasn't even thinking about UFOs at the time!"

Over the following hour, Alfred Burtoo would be asked questions. After being instructed to stand beneath a glowing amber light, the figures asked him his age, and he replied, "seventy-eight on my next birthday!" He was then asked to turn around in the column of light. A further wait ensued until the voice finally called, "You can go! You are too old and infirm for our purpose!"

After departing from the craft, the man returned to where he had been fishing. He then observed a series of lights and moving devices through the trees. Soon enough, there was a loud sound, and the light was gone. Surprisingly untroubled by the incredible events, Alfred continued with what he set out to do and fished throughout the night.

At around 10 am, two MoD police officers approached Alfred and made small talk. When the fisherman mentioned his incredible encounter, the policeman replied, "Yes. I suspect you did see a UFO. I expect they were checking on our military installations!". Soon afterwards, Alfred headed home to bed.

Alfred Burtoo pictured in 1983

The story began to circulate. Alfred appeared in the local paper "Aldershot News". After contact with Surrey Investigation Group of Aerial Phenomena, he met with a man named Timothy Good. Mr Good would interview Alfred many times. He featured his findings in the 1983 book 'Above Top Secret' and stated that he thoroughly believed the claims made by Alfred Burtoo.

Incidentally, aside from his age, Burtoo believed his chronic bronchial problems contributed to his release. Had he had a lucky escape? Or might he have missed out on a journey of a lifetime? Regardless, his health failed over the following years, until his death at eighty on 31st August 1986.

Theories have abounded over the years of other possibilities of the events of 12th August 1983. MoD patrols, The Army and Ghurkhas on night manoeuvres have all featured as possibilities to the strange events.

The area today remains cloaked in secrecy, with armed patrols preventing access to the location. The site in 1983, then open to public access, has now been obtained by MoD and heavily guarded. A local witness described the guards as "Of a special-ops-type nature".

Another strange thing noticed is an almost annual article that appears in the local newspaper around the time of the anniversary of Burtoo's death. It always recounts the incident and then goes out of the way to stress that "it didn't happen!" and that the claims "made Burtoo a laughingstock!"

Make of that what you will.

A newspaper article on the story

Alton

I n the early months of 2020, I boarded a train from Aldershot train station. After bypassing Farnham and the wonderful village of Bentley, the train arrived. My destination that grey morning was the charming market town of Alton.

Alton station holds an air of tradition, and like many Hampshire locations, I visited a charm of its own.

Alton is recorded in the Domesday survey of 1086 as Bolton. The area currently has a population of 18,000 residents and has an incredible history. A substantial discovery of Iron Age coins in 1996 now resides within the confines of The British Museum. Evidence of a Roman posting station exists in the nearby area. The discovery of a 7th-century cemetery during building excavations would reveal an item considered one of the finest discoveries of Anglo-Saxon craftsmanship. The Alton Buckle discovered inside the grave of a warrior now sits in Alton's Curtis Museum.

Notable former residents include Elizabethan poet Edmund Spenser and Georgian novelist Jane Austen. However, my task that day was to locate a resident with a far darker and tragic story.

After a substantial walk-through residential area, I managed to find my bearings. The first location of the day now stood before me.

St Lawrence's Church is situated on Church Street. In December 1643, Parliamentarian troops under the command of Sir William Waller attacked Alton. The town, then a royalist stronghold, witnessed a fierce battle that day. Five hundred of the king's foot soldiers battled against Sir Waller's forces, and the survivors fled to the church when decimated. After a bloody attack, Cromwellian soldiers infiltrated St Lawrence's church resulting in a gruesome victory. It is written that a solitary remaining Royalist named Colonel Richard Boles stood his ground to the end, killing six of Cromwell's troops before his death.

St Lawrence's Church, Alton

After so many years, remnants of the battle exist within the church's structure today. The large, dark wooden doors and entrance to the church bears the scars of musket balls. The conflict between royalist and roundhead troops continues within the church in the realms of the supernatural.

Witnesses have claimed to have heard the ghostly sounds of ongoing battle within the walls of St Lawrence's Church. One witness stated that in 1971 she witnessed the sound of fighting accompanied by the smell of an old-fashioned lily of the valley perfume. Others have also claimed to have felt a sensation of men fighting and witnessed the scent within the vestibule doorway. During my visit that day, the unoccupied church made for a fascinating visit without any supernatural activity.

The church door still bares the scars of battle

Just along the road from St Lawrence's Church sits Amery Street. The former home of 16th-century poet and colleague of Walter Raleigh, Edmund Spenser. A figure wearing a dark suit and tall hat considered Spenser had been sighted in the vicinity. Today, a plaque adorns the front of the building in recollection of the author who penned the famous Faerie Queen before his passing in 1599.

The Crown Hotel is situated on Alton High Street. The 15th-century inn features a suitably terrifying story. Sometime in its history as a coaching inn, the building witnessed a horrifying event. The heavily intoxicated landlord cruelly murdered his dog, launching the poor animal at a wall and smashing its skull. The tragic beast then bricked up within the confines of the pub chimney. Sometime in 1967, workers carrying out renovations made a frightening discovery. The skeletal remains of a dog were discovered after removing a partition. The remains of the animal were buried, and builders filled in the wall. It was after this that the incidents would commence.

The Crown Hotel, Alton

The ghostly noises in the dead of night would startle the pub owners. Terrifying, customers heard agonising barking on several occasions culminating from the location of the pub's fireplace. Whether the ghostly sounds continue today is unknown, I thought I would find out for myself.

During my visit, I spoke to bar staff and three regulars of The Crown that afternoon. The story of the ghostly dog is famous and has been known in various versions throughout the years. All three customers knew of the tale yet insisted that they had never witnessed any bizarre incidents during their time as customers.

Perhaps the ghostly dog has finally found peace like other spectral canines I have encountered along the way. The Ghostly Hound of Barnbougle Castle springs to mind. The famous terrier who played none other than Greyfriars Bobby in the 1960s Disney movie is another. The latter is said to haunt an Edinburgh hospital in the North of the city. The dog had lived in the previous site of Challenger Lodge children's home many years ago.

The fireplace is host to a phantom dog

A short walk from The Crown Hotel is Alton cemetery. The attractive burial ground opened in 1856 and has remained a peaceful and well-maintained location. In 1867, a mere 11 years since its opening, the cemetery would see its most famous interment.

On the warm summer evening of 24th August 1867, a child's body was discovered in Flood Meadow. Identified as eight-year-old Fanny Adams, her family resided in nearby Tanhouse Lane. The severity of the child's injuries horrified those who made the grim discovery and subsequent authorities.

The trail led to 29-year-old Frederick Baker, a local clerk. After trial on 5th December at Winchester court, Baker was investigated and was deemed guilty of the murder of Fanny Adams. The murder is considered one of the most despicable crimes in British history and, even today is challenging to read about in detail.

A vintage image of the grave of Fanny Adams

The grave as it appears today

On the morning of 24th December 1867, a sturdy mob of 5000 ventured to Winchester Prison to watch the execution of Frederick Baker. Before his death, Baker wrote to the parents of Fanny Adams, expressing his sorrow for what he had done "in an unguarded hour" and seeking their forgiveness. After his execution, Artists made Baker's death mask, and his full figure was

16

placed as an exhibit in the Chamber of Horrors at Madame Tussaud's famous waxworks in London the following year.

In 1869, new rations of tinned mutton were introduced for British seamen. They were unimpressed by it and suggested it might be the butchered remains of Fanny Adams. "Fanny Adams" became slang for mediocre mutton, stew, scarce leftovers, and anything worthless. The large tins the mutton was delivered in doubled as mess tins. These cooking pots are still known as Fanny's.

EXECUTION
OF
FREDERICK BAKER.

This morning, the wretched criminal, Frederick Baker, suffered the extreme penalty of the law at Winchester Gaol, for the atrocious murder of Fanny Adams, at Alton, on the 24th of August last. It is satisfactory to state that since his condemnation, the conduct of the unhappy man underwent a total change for the better, and he began to realize the awful condition in which he was placed, and his callous demeanour was changed into one of deep dejection. The prisoner has been assiduously attended by the chaplain of the prison, and to such a state of religious feeling had he been brought, that he fully acknowledged the justice of his sentence. The sheriffs arrived at an early hour. When the operation of pinioning had been performed, the wretched man thanked the chaplain, the governor, and the other officials for their kindness. The procession was then formed, and slowly took its way towards the scene of execution. The cap and rope was adjusted, the bolt drawn, and the prisoner was launched into eternity.

You tender mothers pray give attention,
To these few lines which I will relate,
From a dreary cell, now to you I'll mention,
A wicked murderer has now met his fate;
This villain's name it is Frederick Baker,
His trial is over and his time was come!
On the gallows high he has met his Maker,
To answer for that cruel deed he'd done.

Prepare for death, wicked Frederick Baker,
For on the scaffold you will shortly die,
Your victim waits for you to meet your Maker,—
She dwells with Angels and her God on high.

On that Saturday, little Fanny Adams,
Near the hop-garden with her sister played,
With hearts so light they were filled with gladness,
When that monster Baker towards them strayed;
In that heart of stone not a spark of pity,
When he those halfpence to the children gave
But now in gaol in Winchester city,
He soon must die and fill a murderer's grave.

He told those children to go and leave him,
With little Fanny at the garden gate
He said, come with me, and she believing,
In his arms he lifted her as I now state;
Oh do not take me, my mother wants me,
I must go home again, good sir, she cried:

But on this earth she never saw thee,
In that hop-garden, there, poor child, she died
When the deed was done, and that little darling,
Her soul to God her Maker it had flown.
She cannot return at her mother's calling.
He mutilated her it is well known;
Her heart-broken parents in anguish weeping,
For vengeance on her murderer cried,
Her mother wrings her hands in sorrow grieving,
Oh would for you, dear Fanny, I had died.

The jury soon found this monster guilty,
The judge on him the awful sentence passed.
Saying, prepare yourself for the cruel murder,
For in this world, now, your die is cast;
And from your cell you will mount the scaffold,
And many thousands will you behind,
You must die the death of a malefactor,
May the Lord have mercy on your guilty soul.

What visions now must haunt his pillow,
As in his cell he lays now almost wild,
She points at him, and cries, oh tremble, murderer!
'Tis I, your victim here—that little child'
The hangman comes, hark, the bell is tolling,
Your time has come, nothing can save you.
He mounts the scaffold, the drop is falling,
And Frederick Baker fills a murderer's grave.

3 t

205

Documented coverage of the trial and execution of Frederick Baker

I visited Alton on 10th March 2020. After visiting the locations, I have mentioned, I departed with a feeling of Moribund, a sense of sadness, an underlying feeling that Alton had never fully recovered from the tragedy which befell it so many years ago.

ALTON

A feeling of complete misery swept over me that day and remained for days to come. The underlying threat of the Covid 19 pandemic possibly contributed to this feeling on that grey day. I have visited other Hampshire locations to have suffered similar terrible events, such as Hungerford, Kingsclere and Fordingbridge, all with an underlying dread. Alton was, however, completely different.

It has been reported that her spirit continues to play in the flood meadow where her lifeless body was discovered. Could she have been watching me that day?

Basingstoke

W hile travelling across the haunted realms of Surrey and Hampshire, I discovered many tragic tales. Few, however, compared to the tragedy which befell a Basingstoke resident so many years ago.

One day in 1674, a family member made a tragic discovery. Alice Blunden resided in Basingstoke with her husband, William. Alice was found unconscious and unresponsive. Upon investigation, medical staff discovered that she had been overindulgent in a Beveridge of the day called Poppy Water. The opiate-based narcotic beverage was responsible for sinking her into a coma so deep that when her family summoned a doctor, a mirror placed below her nose failed to detect her breathing.

Holy Ghost Cemetery, Basingstoke

Her husband, William, was absent from the family home and away on business. Authorities refused his wishes to delay the funeral to the hot weather and lack of cold storage. Local undertakers hastily acquired a coffin to carry out the interment. Alice described as "A gentlewoman of sizeable girth", was alas too large for the casket. When the undertakers attempted to bury her, they were forced to use oars to accommodate poor Alice into the coffin (An undignified final descent).

Two days later, a pair of local boys played within the grounds of Holy Ghost Cemetery, South View. The location, complete with ancient ruins, can create an eerie setting even on bright summer days. Although daytime, the two boys cautiously moved as they went home. On the way to the rear exit, the boys were drawn to a sound coming from a nearby wall. A terrifying moaning sound emanated from a newly covered plot. The children ran to their schoolmaster and informed him of the terrible sounds from the cemetery. Instead of investigating their claims, the schoolmaster punished them for telling stories.

A full day later, the headmaster's curiosity would prevail. He travelled to the cemetery and immediately was drawn to pathetic whimpering cries from the grave of Alice Blunden. It would take several hours to organise help to dig up the grave. Mrs Blunden, as could be imagined, was in quite a state when she was finally exhumed. Bruises and blood were visible from trying for days to escape her burial plot, and she was so weakened from the experience that she passed out. Rather than taking her to see a doctor, it was decided that as she had, by now, expired.

The sad legacy of Alice Blunden

Police summoned a guard to attend Alice's grave, but through the night, matters would go badly wrong. Through the night, the weather worsened, and a torrential downpour ensued. The guard gave up his post and hastily retreated to a nearby pub. This time Alice obliged everybody by dying.

When the grave was uncovered the following morning, cemetery staff discovered that Mrs Blunden had awoken during the night and, once inside the tomb, tore her face and hands to shreds in her panic to escape. She was not to be so lucky this second time. Her family discovered that this time, for sure, she was deceased.

Alice's husband brought forward a court case. Though being found guilty of murder was a possible outcome, the doctor's testimony saved those accused from the gallows. The result was a judge's negligence decision, a charge against those responsible for the burial.

As a way of apology, a plague was mounted on the wall above the grave of Alice Blunden. The blue in colour memorial reads as follows.

Mrs Blunden, wife of William Blunden, Maltster
Was buried alive in this cemetery in July 1674
Parliament fined the town for its negligence.

The Haymarket theatre, situated on Wote Street, is a building with a haunted

22

history. The facility opened in 1865 as the town corn exchange. It would serve as a public meeting place until 1910 when it became a roller-skating rink.

In 1925 the building was ravaged by fire but luckily salvaged and rebuilt as a cinema until 1940. The building was then managed by Will Hammer of Hammer Theatre and later Hammer Films, who would remain proprietor until 1945. In 1951 the theatre was renamed The Waverley and remains so today.

The Haymarket theatre has witnessed paranormal activity for many years. An unknown figure was sighted crossing the auditorium even during hours of daylight. Like many theatres and cinemas, it is considered that the spirits are those of previous actors. They continue to perform even from beyond the grave. Many theatres maintain the custom of leaving a ghost light on the stage even while the theatre is closed. The tradition said to appease the long-passed thespians. Some theatres have even been known to leave open seats for the ghosts to rest.

Ghostly attendees still visit the Haymarket Theatre

Basingstoke has its fair share of suitably haunted hostelries. Landlords have experienced the mysterious sounds of barrels rolling about in the dead of night, accompanied by footsteps upon gravel. When staff investigated the strange sounds, they were greeted by the sight of nothing. The White Hart Inn on London Road has existed for over 300 years and holds the title of Basingstoke's oldest boozer.

The White Hart Inn has also witnessed a phantom visitor sighted in the vicinity of one of the upstairs rooms. People who have seen the woman state that she appears to be looking in a non-present mirror and combing her hair. A witness in the 1970s claims to have encountered a blonde-haired woman in the same area, also seen combing her hair, which would dissolve into a spectral mist.

The White Hart Inn, London Road, Basingstoke

Another classic Basingstoke property is the Red Lion hotel. The impressive white-in-colour building features no less than 21 separate reported spirits. The hotel dates to the 12th century and, during this time, has witnessed a suitably terrifying history.

The most prominent and frequently seen phantoms are the three noblemen accused of conspiring against Henry V. They were Lord Scrope of Masham, Richard, Earl of Cambridge and Thomas Grey, and authorities tried them at the Red Lion before their execution at the Bargate. Their ghosts are seen in procession, leaving the front door, and walking to where they were hanged, drawn, and quartered.

As mentioned earlier, evidence exists from a séance that the men's spirits walk the hotel today. They are reliving the events of their treacherous deeds so many years ago. Their mournful, agonising cries manifest the one-time building courtroom.

The rear of the hotel entrance

Another famous ghost to be sighted in The Red Lion is that of an older woman. It is considered that she met her fate in an accident on the stairwell and perished from her injuries. Her tragic spirit continues to walk the very stairs where she tragically lost her life.

A short distance away sits Chequers Road. It is a property on this street that holds a frightening, modern ghost story.

In 2018, a builder renovating a house on Chequers Road discovered an unidentified piece of wood in a crevice. Taking it home to identify it and return it the next day, he noticed an oppressive atmosphere in his home.

He discovered the item was a Victorian police truncheon. Going to bed that night, he, and his partner claimed they heard loud banging in the kitchen but couldn't find the noise source. In the early hours, more banging on the bedroom door woke them.

Terrified, they could again find no reason and returned to bed only for the banging to start again. The builder announced he would return the truncheon the next day, and the banging ceased, so the story goes. The man returned it with no further episodes.

The story of the ghostly truncheon is fascinating. What could be the reason for its haunted history? Could the spirit of a policeman from years ago continue to walk Chequers Road on the beat and fight crime? Could they continue their daily tasks as they did when they were alive? A similar story exists from the dark confines of Edinburgh, Leith docks. In this story, the terrifying apparition of a previous security guard continues to patrol the desolate dockland area.

Bentley

O n a warm afternoon in May, I boarded a train from Aldershot on the Alton line. After the stop for Farnham and some idyllic views of the glorious Hampshire countryside, the train slowed down for the next stop.

I was greeted by a small, vintage yet well-maintained station. I departed the train and proceeded along a distant country road. The sound of the train departing towards Alton made me aware that I was standing alone and in the middle of the Hampshire countryside. My journey to another of Hampshire's haunted locations had begun, but this one dear reader was something exceptional indeed.

After a short while, I stood greeted by open fields and a long stretching wooden fence. Directly to my right stood a rusted metal signpost featuring pointers in two directions. To the left pointed in the direction of Bordon 4 ¾ and to the right Bentley ¾.

The long road to Bentley

For a large part of my life, I have enjoyed the many books about ghosts and the paranormal. A standout moment from the early 1980s was acquiring the Usborne Supernatural World book from my school's book club. The rest, as they say, is history.

The works of MR James, Stephen King, James Herbert and many others all played an integral part in my childhood and growing up. Jumble sales and second-hand shops are the catalyst for discovering new titles, many of which names have now been forgotten in the fog-filled mists of time.

The Arthur C Clarke programs of the 80s and the subsequent books that followed led me to discover many famous haunted stories (who could forget the sinister figure in the car's back seat). However, there was one such author who stood out from the rest.

An English gentleman and expert on the supernatural who produced over 50 ghostly titles. His work would cover paranormal tales of the mysterious British Isles and beyond. A man who investigated and wrote extensively about the infamous Borley Rectory, his house was reportedly home to the rectory's original bell.

I had arrived that morning in the village and home of the legendary Peter Underwood.

The legendary Peter Underwood

Peter Underwood was born on 16th May 1923 in Letchworth, Hertfordshire, to a Plymouth Brethren family. At age 9, Peter would claim to have encountered the spirit of his father, who had died earlier that day.

Over the years, Underwood would become a follower of the work of Harry Price. His studies and countless interviews about Borley Rectory (the most haunted house in England) would earn him the title of an expert on the building and its history.

The legendary author became a long-standing member of The Society for Psychical Research and later Chairman of the legendary Ghost Club for many years. Peter Underwood pursued a life of involvement in the paranormal and things that go bump in the night until his death on 26th November 2014.

It was now time to explore his haunted Hampshire legacy.

After a mile-long walk-through scenic countryside, I arrived at a crossroads. After a short walk, I discovered a charming local pub. A wooden feature by a large signpost stating 'Bentley' in large letters provided a map of the village.

The Star Inn situated on Rectory Road has existed for many years. The charming staff and customers immediately made me feel at home. After explaining my visit's purpose and research for this book, they started helping me directly.

A customer who had worked as a steeplejack in the village for many years set about helping me. To identify the white property in which Peter Underwood lived. He claimed, "If it had a chimney, he would know it for sure".

The one property they all insisted I visit was a short distance away on foot.

A short walk along a country road led me to a grassy path. A raised, overgrown side pathway takes you high above the single-track road and along a steep embankment. A decorated footway crosses the hill and culminates through adjacent trees. Directly beyond this example of idyllic country scenery is Jenkyn Place.

Do ghosts still walk this green and pleasant lane

Jenkyn Place is an 18th Century listed house. Reference to the site appears in The Domesday Survey, which mentions a house named after Janckenese Welle (a well exists beneath the house).

The property was acquired by The Coke family in the 1920s and later sold to The Bladon family in 1997. Since then, the property has served as an award-winning vineyard. Many families have owned the property, including Beale, Lutman and Eggar.

The property boasts an incredible array of documented ghost sightings and unexplained paranormal phenomena. A ghostly woman who has come to be known as Mrs Wagg's has been sighted many times over the last 100 years. Her image is sighted in various sections of the property. She is known to appear on a stairway leading up to the west side of the house.

She also appears on a landing and in an upstairs sitting room. Sometimes she is sighted carrying a candle and moving between sections of the upper part of the house. The spirit is said to be at her most active during the winter months.

The footbridge that leads from the garden of Jenkyn Place and leads over the road also features its ghost. The sight of a tall woman in white has been reported walking through the grass and across the footbridge. However, reports of the mysterious woman in white have been sparse over the last few decades.

The Jenkyn Place Bridge

The final and probably the most exciting haunting is seen on the road outside. There are reports of a phantom horse and carriage travelling near Hole Lane. The spectral vehicle will cease travelling at the entrance to Jenkyn Place. The manifestation, complete with the sound of horses and rumbling wheels, has been documented over the years.

I recall reading of a similar apparition within the grounds of Prestonfield House in Edinburgh. A visitor to the mansion property situated in the shadow of ancient Arthur's Seat claimed that one night the sound of horses and wheels up on the gravel awakened him from slumber. Upon further investigation, the following day, the sight of narrow tracks from a wheel greeted him at the front of the property.

Marelands cottage is an impressive property situated off the A31 road. The building dates to 1660, with views of the Wey Valley and towards historic Alice Holt Forrest. The property features a selection of hair-raising stories from those who have occupied its white and foreboding walls.

Lord Stawell, who lived previously, features a particularly macabre legacy. Reports of 'Wild Happenings, Sexual Escapades and Black Magic' surround his time as the property owner. One part of the building holds the title 'The Haunted Room'.

Documentation tells of the murder of an illegitimate child supposedly at the hands of Lord Stawell. The dead infant is rumoured to be bricked up within the confines of a fireplace within the property. There is a story of a bloodstained hearthstone, the hideous red stain unable to be removed.

The entrance to Jenkyn Place Vineyard

The house developed such a reputation that a previous owner known as

Mrs Joy had the place exorcised by a priest to rid the building of its terrible, haunted past. After the exorcism, the owners claimed to have never re-encountered the hideous scenario.

The property Mr Underwood occupied in Bentley is known as The White House. The building was dated 1742 and was home to Peter and his wife until he moved out in 1999.

During their stay in Bentley, the esteemed ghost hunter claimed to have witnessed a solitary ghost within The White House. A female figure, a Victorian Lady, short and dumpy, standing smiling with her arms crossed. Several visitors to the building have laid claim to witnessing the same friendly spectre.

Upon his departure, the house was owned by Valissa Burnett. The new owner claimed in 2001 to have encountered the returning smell of old pipe tobacco in some regions of the house. Other unusual odours would emanate throughout the building, including the strong smell of smouldering wood fire from a now deserted and unused fireplace.

As my wonderful trip to haunted Bentley ended, I knew I must return. My fascinating conversation with the staff and locals of The Star Inn uncovered many more locations.

I never managed to find the exact location of Peter Underwood's haunted White House and have yet to see the famous Borley Rectory bell. But you can rest assured that one day in the future, I shall certainly be back.

Betchworth

itting 3 miles east of Dorking and 3 miles west of Reigate sits the Surrey village of Betchworth. It is situated on the River Mole and Mole Valley, the village dates to the 11th century. To describe the appearance of anything other than idyllic is an understatement.

A long and winding road accesses the village. Old Road junctions at Sandy Lane and a gatehouse at the foot of the drive sit with a signpost announcing 'Hartsfield Manor'. It is here that my journey and my story begin.

During the early months of 2022, I visited the delightful confines of Hartsfield Manor. The building was constructed in the 1860s by Arthur Woodriff Jaffrey, son of John Richmond Jaffray, a merchant who owned an import-export business, operated in England and America. Arthur joined his father's firm and became quite wealthy. In 1858 at the age of 36, he married his cousin Mary Twynam Woodriff (1841-1885) who was nineteen years his junior.

Unfortunately, in 1864 Arthur had a hunting accident. He was shot in his hand, and after medics removed the bullet, the wound became infected, and he died. Mary, who was pregnant, was left a widow with their three children, Lilian, Edward, and Mary. The couple lived for some time with Arthur's father, who had rented Betchworth House, and in the 1860s, the building of Hartsfield Manor commenced.

An impressive view of Hartsfield Manor

Upon arriving, I was taken by the impressive frontage of the Manor. Unique turrets populate the building's façade while gargoyles and other sculptures welcome you to the entrance. I was there to relax and enjoy the roaming Surrey countryside, but I was also there to discover the ghosts of Hartsfield Manor.

I was greeted with a warm welcome. The reception staff were glad to chat about the history of the building and spend time with me over the following hour. After a while, our conversation moved to the Manor's ancestry. Vintage images and woodcuts adorn the walls of the lower stairwell displaying images of previous owners and families. It was at this point we addressed the other residents, the ghosts. Our guide Tony referred us to another staff member named Louise. She knew a ghost story of two.

Whilst on nightshift Louise noticed a figure pass the reception where she sat. Although the small hours, she is adamant that something bypassed her at the reception. She looked out from the reception booth to see who it was and was met with nobody there at all. The area where Louise states the figure passed leads to conference rooms and a bar. It is a straight passageway with nowhere for anybody to hide. Incidentally, the staff locked the door to the bar.

Interiors of Hartsfield Manor

A bartender I spoke to relayed a similar story, again from the same area and along the corridor towards the conference rooms. On this occasion, he is confident that the passing figure is a lady in a dress with grey hair.

Louise relayed some other known ghostly tales of Hartsfield Manor. When entering the Manor's central doorway, you are greeted by an incredible stairwell. Impressive large windows illuminate the stairwell. Tapestries and pictures from years gone by now surround you. They furnish the walls and the stairs leading to the beginning of the hotel rooms. It is here that the ghostly sight of a black dog has been witnessed. It runs down the stairs and vanishes upon reaching the bottom railing. Staff have described the animal as a hunting dog.

As you depart from the reception and the stairwell, there is a bar directly to your left. It is in the area that another well-known face has been sighted. The figure, 6ft tall, stands at the bar as if he is waiting to be served. Witnesses have described the ghost as a grey-haired gentleman. However, on this occasion, the only grey-haired man propping up the bar was me.

36

A phantom dog is seen running down the stairwell

Ghostly children have been sighted and heard dancing in the middle of the dining room. The reception staff listened to their voices cascading through the drawing room. Other workers witnessed their playful ghostly sounds during the day and night.

The final and most terrifying of Hartsfield Manor's ghosts exist in rooms 34 and 35. The sight of a short-haired lady has terrified guests for many years. Louise recalls

"There is one story about a workman who stayed frequently and always had room 35. On his final visit, he checked out in the morning without speaking to anyone. Later in the day, he sent an email complaining about an elderly lady in the room beside him. She stood over him as he slept in bed and terrified him whenever he fell back to sleep. He never returned to the hotel again."

"We also often have guests report that they have heard strange noises and footsteps at night and ask if the hotel is haunted."

I did not encounter any restless spirits at Hartsfield Manor, but had a wonderful stay. So much so that the image of the building adorns the book's front cover.

The ghosts of Hartsfield Manor

The village of Betchworth was my next destination. A short walk from the Manor and down a country path exit onto Old Road. A short drive away, you arrive at Brockham. It is here that we discover our following ghostly location.

Betchworth Castle is a mostly crumbled ruin of a fortified medieval stone house. In 1798, Henry Peters bought Betchworth Castle and renovated it to be a comfortable family home. Henry lived at Betchworth Castle with his wife, Charlotte Mary Morrison, and his twelve children until he died in 1827.

After Henry's death, Betchworth Castle was not inherited by his children and therefore was bought by David Barclay and later by Lord Henry Hope, who demolished large parts of the castle and left it in ruin, as is seen today.

The road to the village

A tragic story exists from the castle's history. On a dark and windy night, Lord Henry Hope noticed a suspected intruder within the castle grounds. He was presuming the man was an escaped prisoner he gave chase that night.

Lightning flashed, and rain lashed down upon Betchworth that night. Passing through fields, he eventually sighted a shadowy figure by the castle moat. The enraged Lord Hope brought down his weapon and struck the intruder. Aided by the lightning Lord Henry Hope caught sight of the fatally wounded man. To his absolute horror, the body was not that of the escaped prisoner but his son.

The spirit of Lord Hope continues to walk the ruins of Betchworth Castle. His terrible figure, sighted over the years, wringing his hands in despair over the tragic killing of his son.

The ruins of Betchworth Castle

On other occasions, the castle has been plagued by the apparition of a ghostly black hound. Whether it is connected to the spirit of Lord Hope is unknown, yet equally terrifying to all who have witnessed the fearsome spectral animal.

After my trip to Betchworth's haunted realms, I drove back via the A3 motorway. At this point, I recalled a frightening tale from a colleague some years ago.

It all began on a dark December Sunday night in 2002 when a motorist reported seeing a car lose control and leave the A3 around 100 metres before the emergency slip road at Burpham.

Police were called to the scene to search for the wreckage but could not find any trace of a crash until an officer stumbled upon a maroon Vauxhall Astra nose down in a ditch, covered in undergrowth.

However, there was one irregular detail – the car had not crashed recently. It had lain undiscovered for five months, confirmed by the additional discovery of a decomposed body nearby.

The crash site with a mysterious discovery

Hysteria greeted the findings, as an article suggested in the national press that the sighting of the car leaving the road just the night before could only have been a ghostly replay of the fatal crash earlier in the year.

This view was not shared by Surrey Police, with a spokeswoman insisting that the incident had only ever been treated as a regular road traffic collision and that the car was obscured by leaves and branches most probably prevented it from being reported earlier.

She added that even if motorists had spotted the vehicle, they might have assumed it was already being investigated.

Police identified the body from dental records as that of 21-year-old Christopher Brian Chandler. He was from Middlesex and had been on the run since July 16 that year for robbery.

The site of the A3 ghost crash in Burpham

What has come to be known as The A3 Ghost Crash has now become the source of urban legend. During research for this book, I was informed by people I interviewed of similar incidents in Woking, Farnham and Hoggs Back.

However, one thing is undoubtedly true. The story of the Burpham ghost crash is possibly one of the scariest tales I have encountered recently. It rightfully deserves its place within The Haunted Realms of Surrey and Hampshire as a genuinely frightening story.

The next time you drive in your car late at night, the full moon in the sky and the dark road shrouded by substantial trees. Please remember the strange incident that occurred to travellers of the A3 near Burpham in Surrey. Similar tales exist in the likes of The Hairy Hands of Dartmoor and the terrifying story of a phantom lorry sighted in the vicinity of Stow near Galashiels, Scotland.

Please take care. It could be you.

Bramshott

The village of Bramshott is said to be home to 27 different ghosts. This figure alone may count for an astonishing amount of supposed paranormal activity. The small village is precisely this 'A Small Village'. However, with connections of the like I am about to disclose, it may be no surprise that Bramshott may rightfully deserve the title of 'The Most Haunted Village in England'.

My quest to discover the haunted realms of Surrey and Hampshire saw me board a train to the Hampshire village of Liphook. The first records of Liphook date back to the 1200s. A court roll declared a William Lupe in 1281 and a Matilda of L'hupe in 1337.

During the late 1600s, the area would become a coach stop on the London-Portsmouth route. Although the road was initially deemed poor, the path became essential in cutting time for military and travellers. As with many formative byways of the time, some would seek out ways to exploit them.

On the corner of The Square sits a large, white building named The Royal Anchor. The large coaching inn, reportedly constructed in 1588, has a suitably exciting history. The scourge of highwaymen arrived with the coaching age of the 1700s, and the village of Liphook was no exception to their sinister presence.

Records state that Admiral Nelson spent his last night in Liphook and resided in the Royal Anchor before sailing for The Battle of Trafalgar. George 111 and Queen Charlotte also visited the inn. Their stay would allow the name change from The Blue Anchor to The Royal Anchor over subsequent years.

The site of the final battle of highwayman Captain Jacques

The building is haunted by the spirit of a notable highwayman from its past. Captain Jacques is reportedly a smuggler and highwayman of the day. His gang would operate throughout Liphook and nearby Bramshott Village, where it is said they used the church to hide their acquired loot.

On a dark, windy night and after a pursuit by customs men, the infamous highwayman fled to the confines of the Anchor hotel. The customs officers, determined to capture the smuggler, pursued him inside and eventually cornered him on the building's first floor. After a fierce battle, the infamous Captain Jacques met the wrath of the king's men and was gunned down while attempting to escape through a hidden passage. Jacques' days of evading the law were now over, but it would not be the last time Liphook would hear his name.

Room number 6 is where the infamous highwayman would meet his demise. The room, for many years, was used as accommodation. I met with staff from the hotel, and they were very much aware of the legend. Many guests have laid claim to witnessing a dark figure with a pointed hat within the confines of the room and considered to be Captain Jacques. However, nobody has reported anything malevolent associated with his appearance. Staff informed me that while working in other parts of the building, they have encountered a sense of somebody watching them throughout the day and night. Could it possibly be Captain Jacques watching for customs and excise officers and ready to make a sharp exit?

Room number 6 is currently used by staff and management and is no longer used as a room for the public. The hotel manager Sandra and the two bar staff I spoke with confirmed that whenever they have been in the location recently, there have been no feelings of dread of anything untoward. Perhaps The Captain has moved on and no longer recognises the hotel as the coaching inn it once was.

The haunted roads of Bramshott

After a long walk along Headley Road, I stood confronted by a large sign by the side of the road stating 'Bramshott Village'. The long, dark, winding route signalled Tunbridge Lane appeared a decidedly risky affair. Instead, I proceeded along the brighter sight of a public footpath and in the direction of Bramshott Vale Farm. It is here that our first story begins.

A small and ancient footbridge is in the dark shadow of the imposing Bramshott Vale Manor. It is here that a tragic story exists. It is not known if Mistress Elizabeth Butler was an occupant of Bramshott Vale, but it is here that her tale exists.

In 1745 Mistress Butler, after a period of unhappiness, took her own life by drowning in the small stream. An ancient bridge traverses the river, and here that her lifeless body was found on a cold morning. Over the years and on countless occasions, her ghostly figure has been witnessed. She is walking along the side of the riverbank. Her spirit bypasses the small bridge and walks to the bank as she did so many years ago.

On my visit, I walked from the village and proceeded along a long and deserted walkway. The path appears dark even at one o'clock in the afternoon, and the lack of other travellers merely adds to the location unease. After a short while, I would depart onto a path, and soon after, confronted by the stream and bridge. A feeling that I was no longer alone would present.

The path to imposing Bramshott Vale Manor

Across from the path is the start of the village. The view features a grand display of many of its beautiful properties. Between Tunbridge Lane and Church Lane sits a house with an impressive history. The attractive cottage which appears on the corner was the former residence of a certain William Henry Pratt. To those interested in cinema and especially classics of the black and white era, the previous occupant is better known as Boris Karloff.

The legendary actor and star of many of the classic Universal horror movies moved to Bramshott in 1967. The star of the famous Frankenstein movies would create only a few more pictures during his time in the village, including the brilliant Targets in 1968.

Karloff supposedly purchased the cottage due to its location in such a haunted village. He would relay to established author Peter Underwood that a tall figure haunts the house. Although Boris Karloff never witnessed the ghost himself, it is reported that he haunts the building today. On the rear wall of the cottage sits an interesting sculpture. The white bust sits on adjacent Church Lane and is like the late actor. It is almost as if he has never left his final home.

The monster watches over his old house

A village such as Bramshott does not acquire the title of 'The Most Haunted Village in England' without good reason. A multitude of spirits walks the confines of its picturesque lanes and pathways. The spectral figure of a young boy murdered by highwaymen is seen tending to horses as he did when he was alive. The previous site of the infamous Seven Thorns Inn has witnessed a grey lady who is believed to have plunged to her death in the confines of a deep and foreboding well. There are many other stories, but now we focus on a more recent paranormal incident.

Dan Hill is a psychic medium who I have known for many years. Based in Aldershot, Dan realised his talent at a young age. It was while swimming in the Aldershot lido swimming pool as a youngster that something caught his attention. The sight of a man waving to him from the side led him to manoeuvre to the end of the pool and enquire about the man's instructions. When he reached the pool's steps, the man had vanished. Dan's bemused father insisted that nobody had been there the whole time and that he had imagined the incident.

The former home of the legendary Boris Karloff

On a table by the pool foyer sat a tribute to a former staff member and lifeguard. The recently passed man was local and a well-respected staff member for many years. It was the same man Dan had witnessed while swimming in the pool. The man had died a week before the incident. Sometime later, Dan would return to the lido.

On a night in July of 2022, Dan travelled to Bramshott to conduct a paranormal investigation. The warm summer weather aided the group as they walked the moonlit paths of the village that night. Accompanied by a local paranormal group, they would begin as night would fall.

Before he arrived in Bramshott, Dan states that he was drawn to the image of a large tree. Other factors include a young man named Peter, who worked in a mill. There was also the image of a boy, crushed to death at a young age.

St Mary the Virgin Church, Bramshott

After a walk around the village, Dan stated that the logistics of where he imagined the tree to be located were wrong. The tree was absent. The location is directly across from St Mary the Virgin Church. The ghosts of Canadian soldiers reportedly haunt the church grounds. Many of whom died while stationed in Bramshott.

The group continued into the small hours of the morning, and still, Dan remained puzzled by the absence of the tree. Having worked with Dan before in no less a location than the famous Edinburgh Vaults, I have witnessed first-hand, his ability to locate paranormal areas and their spirits. It was then that he realised.

Across from the church sat in the darkness a large wooden bench. The seat has only recently been constructed, bearing the word 'Bramshott' carved into its front. On the side of the structure holds a brass plaque reading the following tribute.

<u>Adrian's Bench</u>
Carved from the oak tree that stood behind you for over 350 years before falling in

March 2018.
Funded by village donations and positioned here on April 14th, 2021.
With gratitude and in loving memory of Adrian Bird of Mallards, Bramshott
1946-2020

Adrian's Bench, possibly a one time gibbet

Could Adrian have possibly been contacting Dan that night? Could he have drawn him to the bench?

Dan also informs me that the tree he had witnessed in his mind's eye was not the sort of tree which would adorn a peaceful village such as Bramshott. The tree he saw was used as a hangman's gallows. The tree's identity as gallows must be confirmed, but Dan and the group remain convinced of a connection that night.

Dorking

I have travelled between Gatwick airport and North Camp for many years. The Reading train commences from the airport and bypasses Horley. The journey is a joy to behold and takes extensive views of Surrey and its chalk-white hills. It is one of these stops that we shall visit now.

On a sunny afternoon in the Spring, I travelled through the flourishing Surrey countryside with a family member. She recalled a couple of stories from the area, stories she remembered from many years ago. The first story concerned the peculiar tale of a man buried upside down on a hill. An interesting tale indeed.

Dorking sits in the shadow of Box Hill. The green and flourishing location contains an incredible story from many years ago.

This story is the strange case of Major Peter Labelliere.

Born in 1785, Peter Labelliere was of French parents who fled to England from France. His parents were followers of the Huguenot religion and suffered massive hardship and isolation due to their staunch religious beliefs.

At age 14, Peter joined the military and rose to Major in 1760. After leaving the army, he would become a political agitator and was accused in 1775 of bribing troops not to fight in the American War of Independence. However, he was never tried for treason.

Labelliere moved to Dorking from Chiswick around 1789, living in a small cottage called "The Hole in the Wall" on Butter Hill and often visiting Box Hill to meditate. With old age, he became increasingly eccentric and neglected his hygiene to such an extent that he acquired the nickname "the walking dung-hill."

On 6th June 1800, the eccentric Major passed away. His bizarre existence ceased, yet his legacy would remain. At the age of 75, Peter gave instructions for his impending internment. His wishes would be that his body is buried upside down on the site of Box Hill in his native Dorking. The area was a favourite of the Major, and he would spend much time meditating upon the hill. His wishes were indeed relevant, but why upside down? Labelliere considered the modern world "Upside Down and Topsy Turvy". His request to be buried inverted in his words would make his resting place right.

For years a small square stone would mark the spot on the top of the box hill of his grave. Sometime during the 1950s, a new headstone would appear. The inscription upon it reads as follows.

Major Peter Labelliere

Aged 75

An eccentric resident of Dorking

Was buried here head downwards

11th July 1800

The desolate grave of Major Peter Labelliere

The story of the eccentric Peter bears a resemblance. It is akin to two other stories I have previously encountered. The strange tale of William Henry Miller, whose giant memorial, The Craigentinny Marbles, rests in an area of Edinburgh. Mr Miller's wishes to be buried beneath the gigantic construction and to be buried face down 40 ft deep have led some to believe his existence as a lycanthrope.

The second instance of strange burial is William Brien, also of Edinburgh, interred in the late 1800s. His solitary lifestyle and neighbours only witnessing him leave his Inverleith property after dark led to rumours that he was a vampire. On the day of his funeral and under strict instructions, the mysterious Mr Brien rests buried 40 ft down, leading to further speculation of his strange legacy. Could Major Peter Labelliere have been hiding a secret as well?

As you depart Dorking Deepdene train station, a long and winding road soon presents. After a short distance and situated between giant trees and shrubs is an impressive property.

The grounds of Pippbrook House date back to 1378. The building was constructed on former manor houses, the impressive property was rebuilt and refurbished in 1859, and Victorian gothic revivalist George Gilbert Scott designed the building.

Throughout its existence, the building has experienced several owners. It has occupied Surrey County Council (Mole Valley District Council since 1974) for eighty years. During the second world war, Pippbrook was used for various duties to support the war effort. Today the building remains as a council office.

Haunted Pippbrook House

The grand building is reportedly haunted. For many years, paranormal activity has been reported, increasing recently after a break-in, resulting in considerable damage. There seems to have been recorded poltergeist activity. Knives are thrown downstairs, and books are heard moving in the library. In one attic room, pens, paper, books, etc., are regularly piled up in the middle of the room. Occasionally a woman has been sighted on the stairs. She is believed to be Caroline Moore, who lived there briefly in the 1880s. The vision of a ghostly butler has been seen looking out of an upstairs window also.

Another interesting fact is that the head of social services is called Alicia (the original owner). She will return regularly after signing in to find her name has been crossed or rubbed out. Perhaps the original Alicia thinks there is room for only one at Pippbrook House.

West Street appears to have quite a collection of haunted premises. The ghost of a lady haunts the commercial premises at number 17. A few doors away, an antique shop called Christique Antiques is haunted by the apparition of a Tudor man referred to as "Ben". He is described as wearing dark clothing or a cloak with a white ruff.

An ancient house exists on the street. It was once the home of William Mullins (one of the passengers aboard the famed Mayflower in 1620). A figure dressed in dark clothes and breeches has been sighted walking up the stairs from the cellar. It has been suggested that this is Mullins returning to his former home.

Does a spirit visit Christique Antiques?

From one side of the street to another is The Kings Arms. I visited this excellent pub on a wet January afternoon. The establishment dates to the 1400s and features the original stone floor. I chatted to the staff about the hostelries' haunted tales, and there are many.

One staff member recalled an incident one day when the pub was quiet. The sight of a pint glass slowly and steadily moving along the bar before his eyes. Seconds later, the barman was startled as an alarming sound caused him to jump from the counter's other side. He described the loud, short sound as spectral.

The Ninth Duke of Norfolk is said to haunt The White Horse Hotel, an old coaching inn. Tenants have encountered him drunkenly roaming the corridors at night, too intoxicated to return to his lodgings at Deepdene House.

I talked to staff when visiting, who relayed their experiences of the time at the hotel. There have been unexplainable instances witnessed throughout, especially in rooms 20, 30 and 37. I asked the staff member if he had ever slept in any of the previously mentioned rooms? His answer being a firm "No!"

The spirit of a woman has also been sighted on the premises of The White Horse Hotel but not for many years.

Farnham

Farnham is a market town in surrey which sits adjacent to the Hampshire border. Domesday records of 1086 refer to the location as Ferneham. The town features a fascinating history of prosperity and tragedy.

The Black Death hit Farnham in 1348, killing about 1,300 people, at that time, about a third of the population. Later in 1625, the area was ravaged by the plague outbreak, leading to economic decline within the town.

Farnham today is a prosperous location and a joy to visit. Many of its ancient buildings and places remain from its history, as do many of its ghosts.

From Aldershot, Farnham is a three-mile journey easily accessible by train and car. As a result, I have been lucky enough to visit many times. The first ghost story I encountered is situated in the confines of Farnham Castle.

A brisk walk along historic Castle Street leads to Castle Hill and culminates at a set of steps. At the summit stands the impressive sight of Farnham Castle. It is here that an array of supernatural stories exists.

The ancient steps to Farnham Castle

Built-in 1138 by Henri de Blois, Bishop of Winchester, grandson of William the Conqueror, Farnham castle became the home of the Bishops of Winchester for over 800 years. The original building was demolished by Henry II in 1155 and then rebuilt in the late 12th and early 13th centuries.

In the early 15th Century, it was the residence of Cardinal Henry Beaufort, who presided at the trial of Joan of Arc in 1431. St Joan of Arc's Church in Farnham is dedicated to her.

Across the moat is a large grass lawn. Directly opposite is a well. It is said that the depth of the well is unknown and that when once furnished by rope, its length is substantial. Here, witnesses have described a "Frightening Form" watching them by the side of the well. The figure has also been reported by the wall and steps leading to the upper section of the castle.

Moving away from the moat and towards the newer section of the castle, you are confronted by large and imposing wooden doors. A sign declaring "Farnham Castle" leads through an impressive hallway and towards a grand, stone stairwell. It is upon these steps the spirit of a man has been seen.

A hooded, grey-cloaked monk presumed to be a Bishop Morley has been witnessed on the stairs and seen slowly gliding down the steps on sunny afternoons. A noticeable difference in this ghost is the sheer solid mass of its appearance. The shape, almost tangible in appearance, will suddenly vanish when observed by whoever is witness to its presence.

The castle entrance from the road

The grand hall of the castle is the location of many reported sightings. One of the more famous apparitions is the sight of a tragic dancing child. The young girl has been seen dancing across the hall. Legend tells that the girl danced to exhaustion for entertainment by owners. Her soul continues to perform, exhausted for evermore. The sound of faint footsteps and a terrible dying gasp have been reported to accompany the child.

It is documented that a visitor to the castle met with a frightening encounter some years ago. The woman states while asleep in an older part of the building, she noticed a slight movement from the bottom of her bed. Presuming it to be a dream, she attempted to get back to sleep.

Soon after, the visitor awoke in terror to the sensation of her bed sheet being slowly pulled away from her. There was nobody else in the room.

When she attempted to pull back the bed sheet and turn on her side, the sight of an unknown figure crouching in the corner of the room caused her to flee in terror. The witness described the shape in the corner and pulling off the sheets as a sense of pure evil.

Leaving the walls of Farnham Castle, we descend the long stretch of road known as Castle Street, a route with no shortage of paranormal tales. I spoke with a shopkeeper on one of my visits to Farnham who had a frightening story.

He relayed the event to me, of the sound of phantom boots heard marching along Castle Street from top to bottom. The man who had lived in Farnham for many years stated that the ghostly footsteps are a well-known story. Although he had worked in the vicinity for many years had never witnessed any instances of paranormal activity.

The legendary author Peter Underwood who lived in nearby Bentley wrote of a nearby haunting of Castle Street. He recalls visiting a small property on High Park Road. The residents reported seeing an unknown male in various parts of the house. Although frightening at times, the apparition remained silent and unmoving. After a while, reports of the man ceased.

Do ghostly footsteps still march along this road?

A selection of Farnham pubs and shops lay claim to events of a supernatural nature. Situated on Station Hill and near the train station is The Mulberry pub. The 18th-century former coach house is a local favourite and has been for many years. Previously known as Blue Boy Inn and now a refurbished gastro pub, the inn has many ghost stories.

The landlord relayed a tale of a resident from Lancashire who occupied an upstairs room for two months that year. The banging sound alerted the publican to head upstairs and check the room. Upon entering, he stood confronted by the guest, frozen with fear and pale, in the corner of the room. His claim of a long-haired figure in black sighted in the toilet left him in a state of terror. The shocked landlord left the room and ventured to the toilet to investigate the man's claim. Upon opening the bathroom door, the landlord met with the chilling sight of the toilet handle swinging by itself. There was no one in the vicinity of the bathroom at all.

The mysterious figure would be sighted over the next ten months. On one occasion, a staff member observed the figure wearing a tall hat and dark cloak manoeuvring through the rear of the pub. When he attempted to follow the man, he vanished around a corner and was gone.

The Lion and Lamb Cafe and restaurant is another spooky location. The property sits in the confines of a picturesque courtyard, and the premises dates to the 16th Century. Its resident ghost is a lady dressed in grey and wearing a suitably large and old-fashioned hat. She is waiting on somebody and disappears when noticed by staff and customers. On more than one occasion, waiting staff have offered the apparition a menu, but she has consistently declined the offer and vanished.

The Lion and Lamb

Farnham Parish Church sits majestically at the end of Upper Church Lane. The attractive cobbled streets and quaint rows of houses paint an idyllic picture of a tranquil English town. Take a walk at 6 pm, and you might be in for a supernatural treat.

The sight of a ghostly female visitor to the church can be observed when the church clock strikes the hour. The ghost is often accompanied by faint sounds of Latin verse from within, even when the building is locked up and absolutely nobody within its walls.

I have sat in the confines of the church and its grounds on many occasions. The faded gravestones and tombs make for interesting reading of the history of the parish church and its many residents. A feeling of gentle tranquillity prevails and is present on even the darkest of days. I have no doubt that whatever may haunt the grounds and walls of Farnham Parish Church is indeed at peace and merely visiting as they may have done many times before when alive.

The author outside Farnham Parish Church

Fleet

T
he small Hampshire town of Fleet was my next destination for The Haunted Realms of Hampshire. It was a damp December day when the train pulled into the station. After passing a busy junction, I began an extensive walk along the long Reading Road. It is here that the search starts, not specifically a search for a ghostly haunted property! On this occasion, something entirely different.

What is now Fleet and Crookham was for centuries an almost treeless and uninhabited heathland that people used to graze animals and cut peat for fuel. Fleet Pond provided fish for the Bishops of Winchester for centuries. Crookham Village is an ancient settlement on the land more suitable for farming, and the villagers attended Crondall Church. Even the opening of the Basingstoke Canal in 1794 had little impact on this rural way of life.

Novelist Rents Haunted House

BRIDGTON, Maine (UPI) — Stephen King, a Maine novelist and author of the best-selling book "Carrie," recently placed a want advertisement for a haunted house in a British newspaper.

It read:

"Wanted, a draughty Victorian house in the country with dark attic and creaking wooden floorboards, preferably haunted."

The unfinished book titled 'The Wimsey'

In 1977 Fleet would welcome a visitor. A famous American author of fantastical books would place an advert in a British newspaper which reads as follows.

"Wanted, a draughty Victorian house in the country with a dark attic and creaking floorboards, preferably haunted"...

The author would find the location he was looking for and, in the autumn of 1977, would move in. However, on this occasion, the British weather that year would prove too much for an American family. The address was Mourlands, situated at 87 Aldershot Road. An attractive detached property located on a tree-lined peaceful road. Incidentally, the author was none other than the great Stephen King.

After the enormous success of his books Carrie and Salem's Lot, King searched for a change. An article from the New Hampshire Nashua Telegraph explains.

BRIDGTON, Maine (UPI) - Stephen King, a Maine novelist and author of the best-selling book "Carrie," recently placed a wanted advertisement for a haunted house in a British newspaper.

It read:

"Wanted, a draughty Victorian house in the country with dark attic and creaking wooden floorboards, preferably haunted."

The King family would get to know the local area and be sighted in local shops. Stephen King would soon commence work on his next book and progress with writing over the coming months.

The legendary Stephen King

In the early months of 1978, The new Stephen King writing project would drastically change. The family leased the property for a year but sadly would only manage three months before facing defeat in the confines of the harsh Hampshire weather. The family would end the property lease early and move back to native Maine.

The book that Stephen King worked on during his stay in Hampshire would never be completed. The working title of the book is 'The Wimsey'. All that exists of the project is the first chapter and a page from the second chapter. An excerpt reads as follows.

In the small segment, we see Wimsey and his driver going to a party at an estate which seems to be in the middle of nowhere. On their way, they have an accident on a bridge seemingly on the verge of collapse. The segment ends here.

I walked along the wet confines of Reading Road for what seemed like forever. I even contemplated return back to the train station and pursuing the following location but fortunately continued. I eventually reached the junction of Aldershot Road. After taking a wrong turn onto a canal footpath, I was soon back on track.

Aldershot Road, Fleet

The street appeared peaceful and quiet, unchanged for decades and solitary in its surroundings. The early January weather would undoubtedly be akin to what Stephen King and his family would have encountered years before, at the beginning of 1978. Rows of large and barren trees line the paths of Aldershot Road, their leaves long departed over the harsh winter months.

Suddenly a property leapt out at me, and I recognised it from my research. I now stood before the very house in which Stephen King once occupied.

The neighbours of Aldershot Road and the property known as Mourlands would appear indeed acquainted with the house's famous history. It took little time before I managed to strike up a conversation with a neighbour on the subject.

The older man recalls the King family living in the area. He informed me that he did see them on occasion, and they were polite and friendly. There was not a significant amount of publicity attached to their stay and the duration of their time in Aldershot Road was fleeting.

The house rented by the King family

I had completed another task. I had walked into the area of another horror legend. It was now time to explore another of Fleet's locations.

A location with a terrifying tale sits on a dark and lonely path, shrouded in dense foliage. The legend of the white lady of Bagshot Lane has existed for over a century. The spectre is considered a local woman, perhaps connected to a nearby farm.

It is recalled that her suicide by drowning happened in a nearby pond. The pond sits beside Bagwell Green Farm and has been the location of several supposed sightings.

Local people have seen a weeping woman dressed in old-fashioned attire. She has been witnessed gliding across the field and over the pond. Upon reaching the bank, her ghostly figure leaves no ripples or disturbance on the surface of the dark water.

A motorcyclist in the late 1960s came face to face with the lady in white one day. She appeared to be sad and walked in the direction of the pond. When the rider attempted to start his stalled vehicle, he noticed the mysterious woman had vanished. He braked in a hurry after witnessing the figure before him.

The road to Bagshot Lane

Godalming

The historic market town of Godalming traverses The River Wey. Dating back to Saxon times, this picturesque location sits within the vicinity of The Surrey Hills. Upon leaving the train station, a grand and imposing white property sits immediately behind you. The building, Westbrook House, is now known as The Meath. The building currently operates as a facility for people with epilepsy and has been used since 1890. The building was previously the home of General James Oglethorpe, who founded the Colony of Georgia in the early 18th century. His inscription and plaque can be seen on the rear wall of the Godalming history museum situated a few streets away.

The building and its grounds are said to host a ghostly figure that can only be seen under the moonlight. The ghost walks across the front of the property and beyond its sprawling grounds. Local legend has it that the spirit is that of Bonnie Prince Charlie. Prince Charles, better known to history as Bonnie Prince Charlie, came to Godalming under the guise of an Italian nobleman.

Did Bonnie Prince Charlie visit under disguise?

As sympathisers of the 1745 Jacobite Rebellion, the Oglethorpe family welcomed the news and enjoyed the company of the elusive, handsome foreigner. Bonnie Prince Charlie would venture into town during his stay, his identity not revealed for many years. His tall frame has been sighted wearing a grey cloak and walking along Westbrook Road and towards The River Wey and in the gardens of the house.

The King's Hotel is situated at 22-25 High Street.

A building has been located on the site of this hotel since the 1300s. The current hotel building has stood since the 17th century. The impressive hotel has seen several famous faces during its many years of trading, including Henry VIII and Peter the Great. Peter the Great is said to haunt this hotel, and room three sees a lot of paranormal activity. Staff and guests alike have heard boots and clothing falling to the floor in this room with no one responsible for the sounds.

Does the spirit of a Russian Czar still visit the hotel?

A resident I spoke to informed me that her mother would babysit for the owners of the Kings Arms Hotel. Once the children were in bed and asleep, she would watch the television, quietly listening to the children. On one occasion, she observed the sound of somebody playing pool downstairs. The building was entirely unoccupied that night.

On another evening, her mother heard beer barrels moving and the lines moving. There was even one instance of a kettle being switched on once again while nobody else was present in the hotel. After these events, the woman decided not to babysit anymore and refused to enter the Kings Arms Hotel.

The first day of my visit to Godalming and The Kings Arms Hotel was a disappointing sight. As I walked along the sunny confines of the High Street, looking for the iconic brick building, I paused upon realising I had walked past the address. I discovered the iconic Kings Arms Hotel unrecognisable and covered entirely in scaffolding. A massive refit was underway, and construction scuppered any chance of a pint in this legendary Godalming haunt. However, all was not lost. I managed to converse with a few builders, busily transporting equipment between the side alleyway and through the building entrance. They kindly took the time to stop and chat with me. One of the builders, a local man, knew the story of the visiting Russian Czar. He had even heard the story of the hauntings but reported that, sadly, he had witnessed no supernatural events so far.

Situated at 132 Church Street is a Godalming hostelry with an incredible history. The Star Inn dates to 1832. The present building dates from the 1700s and remains largely unaltered, delivering a charm all its own. I visited The Star Inn that sunny spring afternoon and met with its landlord Andy.

The incredibly active Star Inn, Godalming

He would recall a selection of the pub's wines, ales, and restless spirits.

Upon entering the Star, you are confronted with a solitary oak wooden bench. Adjacent to the front door, it is here that a figure has been sighted. The spirit is possibly an elderly gentleman in his late 70s or 80s.

A visiting medium informed the landlord that a portal exists in the vicinity of the building where the bench sits. Staff have considered him to be in some way observing the front door. The spirit is guarding staff and customers against harmful spirits.

On the opposite side is an area of the pub known as the snug. The section throughout history has always been referred to as the local area of the bar.

Historic photos decorate the walls, and in the centre sits a large and grand mirror. An older adult witnessed seated directly below the mirror on many occasions.

A staff member witnessed the figure sitting within the snug in one instance.

The startled man, in a panic, ran to get another member of staff. The pub was closed, and it had been entirely unoccupied when he had visited the area a minute before. When both men arrived at the snug, they were greeted with a chilling sight. A recently formed mark on the mirror. Precisely at the same spot where the mysterious man's head rested a short while before.

Another spirit exists in the confines of the woman's toilet. Her manifestation is thought to be attributed to her violent attack within the first 50 years of the pub's existence. The same visiting psychic recognised that the woman manifests the left-hand area of the bathroom, and she was terrified to leave the room.

She cannot leave until somebody releases her.

Andy the landlord in the snug area of The Star

Ascending a broad set of stairs brings you to the upstairs section of The Star Inn. Previously staff accommodation and now used for storage. Staff and customers have witnessed the terrifying spectacle of two children running from one side of the building to the other. Andy recalled an incident from his time as a landlord.

"I was taking stock upstairs to the staff area and stock room. I had an old acoustic guitar which had rested undisturbed against the window at the front of the building.

I was entirely alone when the instrument slowly began to move to my shock. It rocked from side to side against the window ledge, increasing with each second.

Suddenly, the guitar shattered from its neck to the body without warning. The instrument was ruined and unrepairable within seconds of this chilling and unexplainable incident."

Stu and Andy of The Star Inn, Godalming

Stu has worked at the Star for two years. He recalls hearing children's footsteps across the upstairs area of the snug. It was 3.30 am and the conclusion of a memorable staff lock-in. By the time the startled staff member entered the upstairs room, there was no sight or sound. On more than one occasion, glasses have mysteriously launched from behind the bar. They have never harmed a staff member but almost to alert them and ensure they are paying attention. It is practically a rite of passage for staff to experience this alarming incident.

Another member of staff named Freya recalls the sight of a bulbous faced woman standing in the doorway entrance behind the bar. The woman considered to be a previous landlord has been sighted before. The woman stared at her, almost disapproving of her attempts to enter the staff only area. On another occasion, Freya encountered paranormal activity while cleaning the female toilet.

The haunted toilet

"It has happened on several occasions. I have witnessed something attempting to open the door while I am inside. When I checked to see if it was a staff member, I was greeted by nobody in the vicinity of the pub. We will be cleaning up for the night, and I will inform the other staff members that I will be in the woman's toilet.

On other occasions, something within the toilet prevented me from opening the door and leaving. After a while, the restriction shall cease, and the door will open freely."

Jenny, a resident, has frequented The Star over the last thirty-plus years. Her husband worked in the pub in the early 1990s and witnessed several unexplained events during his time. One morning while setting up the pub, the sight of a gentleman in Georgian clothing (possibly earlier) appeared before his startled eyes. The figure traversed through a nearby wall and then through the then location of the bar billiards table. Her husband saw this occurrence on several occasions. Sometimes the figure would stand still and, at other times, travel along the route mentioned. Each time, the one factor was that the figure in the historical period dress was never in a hurry when sighted by the staff of the Star Inn.

Guildford

G uildford is a town with a lot of ghosts. You could write a whole book on this Surrey location, but today we will concentrate on just a few of its stories.

Guildford, sometimes referred to as 'The County Town of Surrey, sits 27 miles southwest of central London. The earliest evidence of human activity in the area is from the Mesolithic. Guildford is mentioned in the will of Alfred the Great from c. 880. The location of the main Anglo-Saxon settlement is unclear, and the current site of the modern town centre may not have been occupied until the early 11th century.

Today Guildford is a bustling university town and one of the most sought-after addresses in the country to live. With no shortage of shops, restaurants and entertainment, Guildford is lively. We begin our story in its pubs.

The Star Inn, Guildford

To any fan of punk rock music, a mere mention of Guildford suggests one band. The Stranglers formed here in 1974 under the somewhat edgy name of 'The Guildford Stranglers. The Star inn hosted the band's first-ever concert in 1974 and remains a popular music venue today. In 2019, the band made an appearance at this famous Guildford venue to unveil a plaque of historical significance.

The Star Inn sits just off the High Street and has existed for more than 400 years. This pub is very much 'The Real Deal. The arches and doorways echo the many revellers to frequent this legendary hostelry. The 100 capacity back room and stage bear the scars of thousands of concerts, but revellers can still hear the distant echo of The Stranglers today. If you find yourself hanging around (no pun intended) late at night, you might listen to some other echoes into the bargain, the chilling echo of distant ghosts.

Still hanging around after all these years

A famous story occurred in 1972. The pub had recently seen renovation work and was now back to regular service. Sometime in the morning, the landlord was alerted. It was the sound of barrels rolling within the confines of the pub. The first thing that sprung to the mind of the shocked publican being, 'Why on earth are they delivering beer at this time? The incensed manager phoned the brewery only to be told they never visit through the night. What was downstairs? The manager proceeded downstairs to the bar and could still hear movement. Presuming the sound of intruders, he prepared to enter the bar. Reaching for the door handle and ready to enter, the stunned man stopped in his tracks. There was now nothing but silence. There was nobody present in the pub.

The area where the bands were performing also witnessed unexplained activity. I recall attending a tribute band of 1970s rockers, ' The Clash,' in or around 2012. The area was icy for a lively concert such as this. The room remains cold year-round.

The final story of The Guildford Star Inn involves that of a smartly dressed gentleman. The figure said to be tall and impeccably dressed, has been seen in conversation with other revellers. He has even been noticed to acknowledge customers by raising his glass.

A short distance away sits an exceptional Guildford tavern. The Royal Oak sits located at 15 Trinity Churchyard. Yes, indeed dear readers, inside a churchyard.

The Royal Oak was built around 1500 as part of the rectory of the holy trinity. The church sits across from its churchyard. In 1870 the church became a hostelry and had remained so ever since. It was owned by George Trimmer, a brewer from Farnham. He created Farnham United Breweries in 1927 and remained a publican for many years.

Many existing features remain today. The original beams and church pillars exist within the centre of the pub. A wooden frame extends beyond the ceiling and continues upstairs with an wooden feature across from the bar. It is here, in this area, that we begin.

The pub by the cemetery

Upon entering the Royal Oak, I was drawn to chalk markings on a dark wooden beam. The rigid section, traditional throughout pubs of this age, runs across the ceiling and culminates at the fireplace. The relevance of the date and the marking's purpose is unknown, but it has remained a tradition for many years. Current landlord Russ (a fellow Scott) informs me that the markings are updated yearly by a group of local Morris dancers each December.

Directly across sits a snug area. Two comfortable sofas and a table occupy the pub corner. A nearby window looks onto an alleyway and then directly towards gravestones. In this location, an older woman's spirit is seen. The figure, sighted in the corner, stares towards the bar, and has appeared on many occasions.

Russ informed me that on more than one occasion, the pub alarm was activated in the dead of night. The beam that triggers the device sits on a shelf and leads to the opposite side of the room. The sensor covers the exact area where the woman has been seen. Russ lives upstairs and states that his dog has growled and pointed to the location whenever the alarm is activated. Upon heading downstairs to investigate the disturbance, each time, he was greeted by nobody else in the pub.

A spirit is often sighted in the corner of the bar

During my first trips to Guildford to research this book, I stopped and asked a passer-by for directions. The woman kindly pointed me toward my following location and had a story of her own to tell me.

The woman had been homeless for the previous few years and camping in nearby woods. The Summer months remained pleasant enough and as a native of the area, she knew her way around. The woods were peaceful, and she remained undisturbed within the vicinity of her makeshift campsite. The calmness of the summer evening passed along as day became night. The evening was now dark, and the sky was clear and crisp.

Through the darkness of the woods, she could hear somebody approaching and footsteps drawing nearer. She stood up and looked outside of the canopy of her tent. There was nobody to be seen. Yet the steady sound of footsteps continued travelling in the direction of where she stood.

She called out, but there was no answer. The footsteps were now a few feet away. Fearful of who it may be, she reached for her torch. She shined the device into the woods. The woman was stunned by the sight of branches swaying in the warm summer air. There was no wind, and nobody was present at all.

Constructed in 1527 upon the site of Whitefriars Monastery, The Angel is a part timber-framed building located on the High Street. Indeed, evidence of its predecessor is still in existence today, the stone vaulted undercroft with remains of the original spiral staircase is said to date from the 14th century.

The name is related to its history as a stop-off point for those travelling on horse-drawn coaches or horseback between London and Portsmouth. It is unsurprising, therefore, to find that the building has accommodated substantial historical figures. Oliver Cromwell, Lord Nelson, Jane Austen, Lord Byron, and Charles Dickens have all rested within its walls. Alongside these famous faces from centuries ago, there is an exciting celebrity tale from more recent times.

In 1973 while filming (possibly Live and Let Die), British actor Roger Moore stayed at the Angel hotel. During the first night of his stay, the actor awoke to discover presumably a man in his room. The figure floated across the room and in the direction of his bed. An icy cold sensation followed, and the figure stopped before him. The actor asked the shape if he could help it, and with this, it vanished through a door.

The same event would occur over the following nights and at the same time, at 2 am. By the third night, the James Bond star would discover a bible open by his bedside. The book sat opened at the 23rd Psalm (The Lord is My Shepherd). That night, nothing occurred, and a good night's sleep would follow.

In the morning, Roger Moore spoke to a maid who enquired if he had slept well. She mentioned the open bible and that the ghost hated the 23rd Psalm. The bewildered actor said nothing.

The same room (room 1) has witnessed spectral sightings for many years. Even today, staff and visitors have reported disturbances in the room. The ghost, presumed a soldier, is seen by many guests. Other spirits reported within the confines of the Angel Hotel include that of a nun and a mysterious spectral butler.

The Angel Hotel where James Bond met a ghostly apparition

On another trip to Guildford, I decided to grab a pint in another of the town's haunted hostelries. The three Pigeons situated on the High Street has existed since the mid-1800s. This historic Guildford pub holds a charm all its own. Its tall glass frontage paints an unusual appearance for an inn of its age.

The Three Pigeons has suffered its fair share of catastrophes over the years. In 1916 a ferocious blaze swept through the building, causing extensive damage. The pub was rebuilt two years later and returned to its former glory.

Records state that the pub first recorded paranormal activity during the summer months of 1976. A famous period in British history as the hottest summer to date, the events inside the pub were, however, served with a ghostly chill.

I spoke with staff about the supposed hauntings. They all agree that the stairwell is the most active section of the pub. There are many ghostly tales associated with the rear stairs of the building. Staff claim that the incidents do not occur when you expect to see a ghost. Not the stroke of midnight or three o clock in the morning, these spirits are more accustomed to dinner time.

The Three Pigeons, Guildford

The staff member has witnessed and heard reports of glasses moving by themselves. He states that he has never had a glass physically smashed but has noticed them move considerably. The light moved by itself when nobody was behind the bar, even without customers being present.

The stairwell leads to a back door and then a garden. A draught has been felt even on warm summer days, always around about dinner time or early evening. There have been reports of animals refusing to pass the stairs in this pub section.

On the day of my visit, I spent some time on the stairwell. I took numerous photographs and waited patiently, but nothing unusual materialized. It was afternoon, and I really should have stayed for dinner.

The final haunted Guildford pub of my travels was the famous Kings Head. This magnificent pub dates to the 1500s and sits in the imposing shadow of Guildford Castle. Upon entering, I was greeted by framed newspaper articles documenting the pub's history, original wooden detail and the warmest of welcomes (there was even a suitably spooky suit of armour in the corner).

Kings Head interior

Upon informing the staff of the project that would later become this book, they were delighted to relay some stories. "The Kings Head is the most haunted pub in Guildford", the barmaid stated. A statement which filled her with pride. Not only is it the oldest pub in Guildford but one that continues to witness paranormal activity today.

She took me aside and pointed me in the direction of the window where the suit of armour was situated. She informed me that this was the location where the ghost of an older woman had been sighted. The basement cellar is another hotspot for activity. She mentioned a feeling of eyes upon you while being down there, especially when the pub is busy. It is not a continuous feeling that catches you off guard when you are active and least expect it.

I sat down directly across from the area by the suit of armour for a while and enjoyed a fine local ale (complete with an old-fashioned, rounded tumbler). The atmosphere is pleasant, and you cannot deny the feeling that you are in the vicinity of something rather special. The King's Head reeks of atmosphere, an authentic Olde English tavern, full of character and a joy to visit.

The Kings Head, Guildford

A short walk from the King's Head and up a steep hill takes you to historic Guildford Castle. The Castle was built by William the Conqueror shortly after the Norman invasion of England in 1066. Used as a Royal Palace, a prison and a private residence, Guildford Castle and its grounds were sold to the Guildford Corporation in 1885. The grounds at Guildford Castle opened as public gardens in 1888 to mark Queen Victoria's Golden Jubilee in 1887.

Today the Castle and its grounds are maintained and operated by Guildford Borough Council and are open to the public daily. A trip to the castle summit will provide you with breathtaking views across Guildford and beyond. On the way down, you may bump into one of the ghosts of the Castle.

It seems to be these renovations that have stirred the slumbers of the Castle's oldest residents. In recent years, there have been several reports that visiting families have come running out of the Castle's ground floor carrying near hysterical children. These children have described witnessing an emaciated figure chained to the castle walls. Chillingly, the apparition was sighted in the part of the Castle used as a prison for those incarcerated accused of severe crimes such as murder, and any prisoners would await their execution there if found guilty. None of the children, of course, would have been aware of this.

Sometime in the 1980s, a separate paranormal encounter would occur. An incident documented by a castle employee states that at the end of a working day, a staff member approached the motte to close the Castle for the day. He was surprised to see a public member inside and stood within the gardens he had just locked up.

He approached the figure, described as wearing a peculiar, Victorian dress. Eager to return home, he unlocked the gate and proceeded towards the woman to ask her to leave. When he reached the gardens where the woman had stood, he was presented with space and nobody to be seen on the grounds of Guildford Castle.

In the shadow of Guildford Castle

Our final trip to the haunted realms of Guildford takes us to historic Losley Park. It is located 3 miles southwest of Guildford in Artington. The More-Molyneux family acquired the estate at the beginning of the 16th century.

The estate has featured in television and cinema, including hit tv shows The Crown and Midsomer Murders. It also featured in the 1978 horror film

The Legacy. Our first story is a fitting tribute and a horror story all its own.

I interviewed a woman called Georgia who has worked for a care company for a few years. The company offices are based on the grounds of Losley Park and inside Losley House. One evening after finishing her shift, she exited the building and locked up for the day. On the way to her car, she noticed a woman on the adjacent side of the car park, watching her intensely from afar.

Georgia noticed that the woman was dressed in bland and old-fashioned clothing. A long brown skirt, green top and light-coloured hair. Her complexion was also ashen, ghastly, and white. The woman did not move but continued to stare, a stare of complete anger.

Georgia opened her car and nervously fumbled for her bag. She was aware of the woman watching her from the rear window of her car. She was now getting closer. In a panic, Georgia continued searching through her bag and eventually found her phone. Exiting the vehicle and looking in the woman's path, she had vanished. Who was the mysterious woman that Georgia met that day?

Three ghosts have been reported from the confines of Losley House and its grounds. The ghost of a smiling lady dressed in Victorian clothes is seen outside one of the bathrooms in the house. The present owner who saw the woman later found a portrait of the ghost in the attic. She is thought to have once lived there herself.

Another ghostly lady has been seen by one of the owner's daughters. This time the ghost was that of a little old lady dressed in grey. She appeared only to the young girls in their playroom, where she would sit and smile at them as if she was taking care of them. As the girls grew up, they realized there was something 'odd' about their friend and told their parents. The family eventually became very nervous about the ghost and left the house.

Losley House of yesteryear

Another ghost has been seen, but this time dressed in brown and does not appear nearly as friendly. The woman has been seen standing at the bottom of the stairs, and when she appears, witnesses usually feel a coldness surrounding them.

As the story goes about 400 years ago, the 'Brown Lady' murdered her stepson by chopping off one of his legs so her son could inherit her husband's fortune. When her husband found out, he locked her away and kept her there for the rest of her life. Every year, on a particular night, horrific screams are reputedly heard coming from the room where she was kept, prisoner.

Could this be the exact ghostly figure that Georgia encountered that day?

Hartley Mauditt

The village of Hartley Mauditt sits one mile south of neighbouring East Worldham and two and a half miles southeast of Alton. The attractive Hampshire village rests in pleasant and calm surroundings. The one dividing factor here lies that Hartley Mauditt sits entirely abandoned and has done for hundreds of years.

A drive through nearby Selborne leads to a stretch of narrow, winding country roads. Upon entering a clearing, the village presents. All that exists of the once great location is a small church and pond.

The road to the haunted village

The church was built between 1150 -1200 and had a suitably exciting history. A series of memorials feature within the Stuart family, whose Manor House stood next to the church before it was demolished. Local tradition says that the lord of the manor, Nicholas Stuart, defended the house during the English Civil War. Roundheads, fighting around the nearby town of Alton against a troop of Roundheads, came and destroyed it. Whether this is true or not, after the Restoration of Charles II as monarch, Nicholas Stuart received his lands back and became the first Baronet of Hartley Mauditt. Evidence suggests that the story is accurate, and for his loyalty, the King restored his land to him. He returned and rebuilt the house.

Church interior

The Stuarts continued to hold the property for several generations until it passed into the hands of the Stawell family. Another local story tells us about Lord Stawell, who loved town and city life, but his country-loving wife preferred to live in the country at Hartley Mauditt. In a rage, it is said, he pulled down the house to prevent her from living there. Whatever the truth, its staircase found its way to Alton council offices, floor tiles turned up in the floors at Colmore Rectory, and it is thought that the round tower, attached to a nearby cottage, was also once part of this old building.

Remnants of its cellars remain, wooded over and stories of a passageway linking the house to Selborne Priory. Many local tales abound of hauntings.

The name of the origin of the settlement is disputed. The family who initially held title over the lands was considered French and called 'Maldnott'. The village close to the church was long abandoned. The outline of buildings can be seen at certain times of the year. A large village pond remains to remind us that the truth about the church and the land around it remains a mystery.

The abandoned village of Hartley Mauditt

The village has a pleasant atmosphere even on the darkest of days. The still water of the pond rests calmly while the distant sound of bird's echoes across the Hampshire countryside. When night-time arrives at Hartley Mauditt, so do its ghosts.

Over the years, witnesses have laid claim to see a startling sight. The ghostly apparition of a phantom horse and carriage has been recorded several times. The ghost is seen travelling at frantic speed up the drive and towards the one-time location of the manor house, only to bypass the pond and then vanish out of sight.

Visitors have also reported the sound of enchanting singing emanating from within the church confines. The sounds of a choir singing during the day and night have been reported. On occasion, the sound of a full complement of singers has startled those bypassing the area, only to be met with silence upon entering the long-abandoned church.

Whether the bizarre sights and sounds connect to the Stawell family is unknown. The manor house, now long gone, and the once active community of Hartley Mauditt now exists purely as a ghost village. Another echo of the haunted realms of Hampshire.

Kingsclere

O n a crisp winter morning, I found myself back in the sunny confines of Basingstoke. The Hampshire town features in this book and has many worthwhile, ghostly tales. My task today was to venture outwith Basingstoke and deep into the Hampshire countryside. Today I would visit a village with an exceptionally dark past.

A short and pleasant bus journey would follow. My destination that morning sits nine miles west of Basingstoke. The glorious views of the roaming countryside made for an enjoyable trip, and soon enough, it was time to depart. The bus pulled up at the side of the road, and I was presented with a charming sight. I had arrived at the village of Kingsclere.

Kingsclere can trace back its history as belonging to King Alfred in his will between 872 and 888, the 'clere' possibly meaning 'bright' or 'clearing'. A local legend exists from 1204 involving King John. While during his stay at a Kingsclere Inn, the king became aware of a bedbug in his room. When The King was prevented by fog from reaching his lodge at Freemantle Park on Cottington's hill, he ordained that the church should erect and evermore maintain upon its tower a representation of the creature that had disturbed his sleep.

The appearance of the village is attractive and preserved in time. The street from the bus stop to the square recalls the village from the screen adaptation of the John Wyndham classic 'Village of The Damned'. The buildings with their original features remain unhampered by time and nestling within the confines of this sleepy location.

I was standing on George Street. On one side of the road sits a beautiful church. As its appearance suggests, St Mary's Church is Norman (12th century) in origin and is a building of significant historical interest. There has been a church on the site for over 1000 years. The present church is built on the site of a former Saxon church.

Across the road sits Falcon House, previously the Falcon Inn. The former coaching inn served its last pint in 1950 yet continues to maintain a charm all its own. The Crown public house is direct across the road and is still open today.

An old image of The Swan, Kingsclere

Just before closing time on October 5, 1944, 10 American soldiers with a US army engineering unit broke bounds and headed to the Crown pub, where they were stopped by regimental police and instructed to return to camp.

They hitchhiked back to their base at Sydmonton Court and armed themselves with rifles and ammunition before returning to the village to seek revenge.

The men searched the village pubs before ending up outside The Crown, where they took up position in the churchyard opposite to wait for their targets to leave.

Coming out of the pub, Private Anderson and another regimental police-man called Brown were confronted by the men armed with rifles, and bullets were unleashed on the pair, hitting Anderson in the chest but missing Brown, who dived back inside.

Anderson managed to get up and run to the corner of the road, where he collapsed in a garden and died between two beanpoles.

Bullets fired through the pub's windows, smashing the frames, and revellers quickly fell to the floor in terror while others threw themselves underneath the bar billiards table to take cover.

The men entered the pub firing their rifles and killing another two – Private Coates and landlady Rose Napper whose husband dragged her to the ground when the shooting started, but a ricochet bullet passed through her left cheek, through her tongue and out through the right of her neck. She died at Newbury Hospital.

A statement from Nelson Miles of the Dell, Kingsclere, said he was in The Crown with his brother Harry and some others that night.

He described the moment shots came through the windows: "I dashed for cover, first getting under the table, then under a seat. Shots seemed to keep on flying past. I then heard Mrs Napper scream. I had seen her standing behind the bar. I lay still until all was quiet, and when I came from under cover, I saw Mrs Napper lying on the floor, bleeding profusely from a wound in the jaw."

Frank Butler, who threw himself to the floor, described the scene as "like hell let loose."

The first suspect was caught by 3 am, and by October 17, military police had rounded up all 10.

Nine were sentenced to imprisonment for the whole of their natural lives, and the 10th was given ten years.

KINGSCLERE TRAGEDY
Three Dead In Hotel Shooting Affray

Mrs. Rose Amelia Napper, wife of the landlord of the Crown Hotel, Kingsclere, and two American soldiers are dead as a result of a shooting affray outside the hotel late last night.

Police are searching a wide area for two American coloured soldiers who are reported to be armed.

It is understood that a disturbance took place outside the hotel late last night and that U.S. military police were summoned.

Several shots rang out. One of the Americans was killed instantly, the second died soon afterwards, and Mrs. Napper died in hospital early to-day.

It is believed she was hit by a bullet which entered the hotel through a window.

It is stated that the troops concerned in the disturbance were all "coloured" Americans.

A newspaper article on the tragedy

Following the massacre, General Eisenhower sent his second in command to apologise personally to Kingsclere villagers for the incident, which was one of many similar to be kept quiet during the Second World War.

Kingsclere residents have a permanent reminder of the bloody massacre, with the gravestone of the landlady in Ecchinswell Road Cemetery, which reads: 'In loving Remembrance of Rose Amelia Napper. Sweetest memories.'

Is there a supernatural connection to the story?

I spoke with three different people during my visit to Kingsclere. The tragic story is now but a distant memory. The staff of The Crown, although aware of the events, are rarely asked about them. An account, however, exists from many years ago.

Stories persist of mysterious rifle fire being heard and sightings of ghosts in the immediate area during the following years. The man I spoke to recalls a tale of a ghostly apparition sighted in the graveyard directly across from the Crown. It is unknown who or what it may be or if the spirit has any connection to the tragic events of October 5, 1944.

Reigate

I have observed the same notifications over the train tannoy for many years of traversing the train journey from Gatwick to North Camp. "The next stop will be Redhill, Horley, Gomshall" the voice relays. Today I was getting off at the next stop on the line. What did these lesser-known areas hold for me? Did they have ghost stories, perhaps a mysterious haunted house?

Today I was visiting Reigate.

Reigate has the classic appearance of a traditional British railway station. It is frozen in time with a taxi rank and classic English pub to serve the weary traveller. Take a right at the top of the road, and it will take you onto the route of the A27 (other adventures would materialise on this busy stretch of road). Take a left and cross the railway crossing, and you are heading in the right direction for an abundance of ghostly tales. Head along London Road for a stretch, and not before long, we are presented with a long and imposing tunnel. The area popular with local students is the one-time location of a local market. It is also the start and entrance to the fascinating Reigate Caves.

Reigate Tunnel entrance

The underground network of caves is, in fact, two sets of mined tunnels, excavated initially for the extraction of silver sand and used primarily for glassmaking. The East Mine has seen subsequent use as a munitions store in World War I, beer, and wine storage and as a World War II Control Centre. The West Mine was also used for storing wine and beer and was an air-raid shelter in World War II. Part of it is now used as a local club's rifle range. Both mine sites were developed after the cutting, and the tunnel through the hill was constructed as part of the new road and tunnel that opened in 1823.

The eastern side was initially excavated to provide storage space for the local brewery. It was integral storage connected directly to a local hostelry's back. It has now been converted into a self-guided museum that covers the local history of the site and some of the other local hearthstone and sand mines. The caves feature as a location for visitors over the summer months. Guided tours take visitors throughout the vast network deep within the Surrey landmark. The question, however, remains,

Has anybody met its ghosts?

The ghostly Reigate Caves

That day, my contact (and guide) assured me that the caves play host to much paranormal activity. Having taken part in tours recently, he has not only heard tales of ghostly sounds but has claimed to have witnessed a first-hand account. While on a walking tour, he claims to have sighted a shadowy figure standing behind a pillar. The other group members were already moving towards the following location when something caused him to pause and wait a while. Something was watching him from a pillar. The area described by him as non-descript held him in a grasp of paralysis but only for a short moment. It was almost as if somebody sought his attention before suddenly disappearing before his eyes. He states that he wasn't scared but curious about what may have been wanted before him.

He states that he has heard a story of a paranormal group who spent the night in the caves. During their overnight investigation, a table was tipped, and a group member was knocked to the floor by unknown forces. It is a shame that the cave tours have ceased operation. Hopefully, they may resume soon, along with the highly rated Reigate Ghost Walks (I enjoy a good Ghost

Walk, you know).

Travelling above the caves, you are presented with the impressive site of the remnants of Reigate Castle. Although the original castle is now long since gone, the replacement gateway dates to 1777. A short distance away is the site of Knights Department Store. The white in colour building sits on Bell Street and is now an Oliver Bonas shop. It is written that the shop is haunted by the spirit of a small boy named Tommy. The youngster was believed to be murdered on the site when it was once a hotel.

The previous site of Knights Department Store

I have read of the following Reigate location in a selection of books, and this day was a joy to be present on its grounds. After a hearty walk along, what appeared to be never-ending country paths, I stood confronted with a long, broad approach. The area appears dark and secluded by a sprawling barrage of branches and dark on even the brightest days. The location is perfect for a Surrey ghost story, and I was certainly not disappointed. The fantastic view of St Mary's Church stood before me.

The first story I encountered concerned a Sunday service with a difference. A parishioner walking near the church was impressed that day by the glorious sound of singing. Presuming the choir to be in full swing, the man stood puzzled to witness the doors locked. Upon further investigation, the bemused man was shocked to discover nobody in the building that day.

The spirit of a small girl has been sighted close to the vicinity of St Mary's Church. A busy road separates the path leading up to the church entrance. The end of the track is decorated by what appears to be a military pillar box. It is here that a ghost child has been sighted. Did she meet her fate on the busy road? Is she connected to the ancient cylindrical construction? I had to venture inside the church and find out for myself.

I spoke with an American woman who was visiting the church that day. She knew the story of the choir singing and the spirit girl of the lane. She mentioned that both tales were well known to people of the area and that if I was to head along on a Sunday, parishioners might furnish me with further ghostly tales. I might do that.

St Mary's Church

I returned to Reigate a few months down the line. On this occasion, I was not venturing into the town centre but seeking a bus to take me to the small village of Pyrford. With British horror movies being another suitable passion, I ventured that day to discover the location of one of my favourite British horror films. Scenes from the 1976 movie The Omen were filmed at Pyrford

Court. The setting of the tragic demise of the family's nanny, only to be replaced by the suitably malevolent Mrs Baylock, was filmed on the grounds. It took little time to locate Pyrford Court, and I was also informed that it had been featured in Tales from the Crypt and Psychomania (two other favourites of mine).

At the front of the building is a large rock. It is here that a local legend exists. The Pyrford Stone has various aspects of folklore associated, and one myth is that when it hears' the cock crow at dawn or every night when the clock of St Nicholas' church strikes twelve, the stone will turn. The tale is odd since St Nicholas' church has never had a clock face.

The Stone at Pyrford Court

On this day, as I was taking pictures of the stone and minding my own business, I was nearly wiped out by a speeding vehicle. To put you, the reader, in the picture, Pyrford Court is in the absolute middle of nowhere, it has no pavement, and the bus stop is the only safe means of protection from traffic. Could the much-documented Omen curse have been monitoring me that day?

Weybridge

There have been ideas for books that I have started and yet never completed; one day, I hopefully will. One such project was a collection of locations from classic British horror films. Books have been released on the subject before, but this will be my own collection, which has been a long time in the making. Another visit to an incredible haunted Surrey location brought me to one such place.

The Amicus portmanteau movie 'The House That Dripped Blood' was unleashed upon the public in the glory days of 1971. One of the sections of the film features a gaunt looking, recently widowed Peter Cushing. In the story, the haunted protagonist grieves the loss of a long-lost flame. He walks a quaint English town's streets, shops, and churches. It is here that we visit now and a location with some very real hauntings.

Weybridge sits on the river Wey and bounds to the north by the Thames at the mouth of the Wey. Weybridge appears in the Domesday Book of 1086 as Webrige and Webruge, held partly by Chertsey Abbey; partly by an Englishman from the abbey; and partly by Herfrid from the conqueror's brother, the Bishop of Bayeux. Until the late 18th century, Weybridge was a small village with a river crossing.

Elmbridge Museum is on Church Street above the library and has a range of exciting exhibits, including artefacts from Henry VIII's Oatlands Palace, which used to stand at Weybridge. In 1537, a manor house affiliated to Weybridge, on what was a border of Weybridge and Walton, Oatlands Palace, was built by Henry VIII, which was where he married his fifth wife, Catherine Howard. When it was demolished in 1650, bricks from its walls helped to line the then-new Wey Navigation Canal.

Weybridge holds the accolade of being the home of formula one motor racing. Brooklands, the first purpose-built motor-racing circuit in the world, opened in 1907. Constructed on farmland south of Weybridge, the concrete track was designed by Capel Lofft Holden and had a total length of 2.75 mi (4.43 km). The first races for motorcars took place in July 1907 and for motorcycles in February the following year. Both attracted many entrants from across Europe, and by 1911, the British Automobile Racing Club had established a programme of regular race meetings. The large track has a reputation as a top-class racing circuit and continues today. It also features its very own ghostly tales.

Brooklands Race Track, 1932

The haunting started after Hugh Locke King opened Brooklands Motor Course. One involves Percy Lambert, a racing driver who died on October 31, 1913. Percy was due to get married later that year and therefore promised his fiancée that he would give up racing. Unsurprisingly, due to Peugeot beating his original record, a few months later, he decided to get behind the wheel again to make another attempt – sadly dying in an accident caused by a burst tyre on Brooklands racecourse. Spiralling through the air and landing with force, in a car with no protection, well beyond stopping speed, Percy passed away as he was rushed to hospital.

The legendary Percy Lambert

Whilst Percy Lambert is Brooklands' most famous ghostly visage, there have been reports of others – many of which are far grislier. There have been numerous sightings of a ghost in a complete racing kit – leather coat, cap, and goggles pacing the track and strolling into a large hangar – known as "The Vatican" – where Percy used to store his Talbot race car. Other sightings claim to have seen him racing his vehicle along the now-disused racetrack, sometimes accompanied by the roar of an engine.

A young local boy needed medical treatment following a run-in with a man staggering around with a semi-dismembered head hanging off. It is believed that the man could be Captain Toop – who crashed in a Peugeot in 1924.

Ghosts of aviators and ground crew who worked at Brooklands during

World War 2 (when it was converted to accommodate the RAF and disguise the track so that the German pilots had no landmark to identify their location) have been encountered.

Reports in the early hours of the morning of hearing cars roaring along the racetrack and the sounds of crashes – including splintering wood.

Percy is buried at Brompton Cemetery in London in a streamlined coffin – curiously morbid, given that it was built to resemble the car he died in…! His epitaph reads:

"A modest friend, a fine gentleman and a thorough sportsman. The first man to cover one hundred miles in one hour. Killed by accident at Brooklands Motor Racing Track whilst attempting further records. October 31, 1913."

The tragic tale of Percy Lambert has echoed through the writings of several authors. The 2016 novel 'The Ghost at Brooklands Museum' by Mark Richardson sees a fictitious family move to a property close to the track, only to witness the phantom racer in all his ghostly glory.

Another witness has recently relayed a story from the 1980s. Between 1984 and 1987, he would visit the remnants of the racetrack with his friend. They would cycle around the circuit and enjoy themselves without a care. He recalls.

"On this particular day of Brooklands Racetrack pillaging, my friend was out about 100 yards from me, kicking cans around, and I was at the entrance of a yet-to-be-explored bunker.

"It had a concrete staircase down to a very dark space below. As the nosy parker, I had no idea what was down this staircase and started to descend the steps."

"Well, I must have gone down about ten steps or so when suddenly, an awful, terrible gust of icy air came up from the cavern. It was not the cool, refreshing air you feel while going underground on a sweltering summer July day but the most bone-chilling, evil vibe."

"I almost fell due to my shock."

"I raced up those stairs, eyeballs bulging and screamed to my friend, "Let's go!!! Now!!! I mean it!!! Now!!!"

"We ran as fast as our 13-year-old legs could carry us, up that steep slope, over the fence and didn't stop till we got to the railway tracks."

"There had not been a soul around, not even a bird. Someone or something was there!"

"I will never, ever forget it."

The race track as it appears today

Oatlands Park Hotel has existed as a hotel since 1856. However, the previous mansion house and grounds date back to 1537 and have connections to many famous historical names. In 1794 the mansion was burnt down and was quickly rebuilt in the Gothic style of the period. In 1846 the estate was broken up into lots for building development and sold at three public auctions in May, August, and September of that year. Following a period of private ownership by James Watts Peppercorne, the house became a hotel in 1856, known as the Southwestern (later Oatlands Park) Hotel. From 1916 to 1918, during World War I, the hotel was used as a hospital for New Zealand troops injured in France.

I travelled to Oatlands in the Spring of 2016. The plan that weekend was to stay a couple of nights, indulge in fine dining and meet the ghosts of the building. Upon arriving, I stood confronted by an imposing high tower. This site is where a serving maid leapt to her death from the bell tower. She landed in the vicinity of room 1313, and it is here that she is still witnessed today. Guests have reported sudden drops in temperature, and one guest on the trip adviser claimed to have captured a chilling recording in the dead of night.

Oatlands Park Military Hospital 1916-1918

During the 2015 Rugby World Cup, the Welsh rugby team stayed at the hotel, occupying fifty of its 144 rooms. Some players claim to have witnessed the ghost of King Henry VIII while staying at the hotel. The story gained media coverage, and several players provided interviews while others insisted that their fellow teammates were merely dreaming.

During my stay, I ventured to the Tudor wing and room 1313 to take photos for this book, only to be asked not to be the front desk staff. However, the room I stayed in had a suitably spooky atmosphere, and it was not even inside the building. The room looked across a large pond. The sight and sound of woodpeckers flying over the pond caught my attention all weekend. The distinctive sound of the woodpecker became commonplace, and I soon became used to it.

The view from my room

At 3.30 am, I awoke to somebody walking on the grounds outside. I looked out of the open window and could see nothing. However, the sound of somebody moving close to the pond continued, yet nobody was there. The incident was innocent and perfectly explainable, yet the following factors were present. It was May 14, the sky was light, and the pond and grounds were visible. The sound materialised directly before the window, yet nobody was there. The atmosphere was unnerving and caused me to close the window for the rest of the night.

I enjoyed my stay at Oatlands Park Hotel and recommend it to everyone. Having stayed at many comparable properties with suitably haunted histories, Oatlands deservedly joins the ranks of the haunted hotels of Surrey and Hampshire.

Woking

"Slowly and surely, they drew their plans against us".

Sometime in the late 1970s, I would encounter the cautionary voice of Richard Burton relaying a warning to all humanity. These words would deliver as the catalyst to terrorise over a century of listeners. I was one of them! The glorious double album musical version of HG Wells' The War of the Worlds was essential listening of the time.

The story penned in 1897 by the celebrated author of science fiction classics such as The Time Machine would terrify many. Listeners shunned the piece for many years due to its cause of moral panic (an early predecessor to The Blair Witch Project, for sure). In 1938 a radio broadcast voiced by actor Orson Welles caused listeners to flee to the streets in panic due to its news broadcast delivery.

The frightening story of a martian invasion of earth would appear in several different formats. From stage, print and eventually, to the cinema screen, The War of the Worlds would leave a lasting impression upon the world, but where exactly was it set?

The leafy Surrey town of Woking sits 22 miles from Central London. Evidence discovered states the area dates back to the Palaeolithic and Bronze Age periods. There are examples of Roman occupation in older sections of Woking, including Old Woking and Mayford. Visitors can find Roman tiles in areas of the tower in St Peter's Church.

The town would become a prosperous area with an economy and industry connected to the River Wey and Basingstoke canal. In 1834 the construction of the London and Southampton railway would commence and with it began our first story.

In the first half of the 19th century, the population of London more than doubled. From a little under a million people in 1801 to almost two and a half million in 1851. Despite this rapid population growth, the amount of land set aside for use as graveyards remained unchanged at approximately 300 acres spread across around 200 small sites.

Spirits served here, the train to Brookwood Cemetery

The difficulty of digging without disturbing existing graves led to bodies often stacked on each other to fit the available space and covered with a layer of earth. In some cases, large pits were dug on existing burial grounds, excavating the previous graves, and fresh corpses were crammed into the available space. Even relatively fresh graves had to be exhumed in more crowded areas to free up space for new burials, their contents being unearthed and scattered to free up space.

A parliamentary act was passed in 1852 as a direct result of the over-crowding and burial problem. The London Necropolis Company (LNC) was formed. With the formative years of the railway, the local authority decided to create a railway line to transport London's dead out of the city and to a newly constructed Cemetery.

The journey to Brookwood need not be unpleasant. Brookwood Cemetery opened in 1852 and was consecrated by Charles Sumner, Bishop of Winchester. Upon the Cemetery's opening, it would not take long for the interments to begin and not before long, Brookwood Cemetery would become the largest Cemetery in the land.

A dedicated platform would operate from London Waterloo station transporting the deceased and their families directly to the Cemetery. It is recorded that the train would provide a full range of drinks and refreshments. A sign boldly states at the bar, "Spirits Served Here".

The sign that marks the spot of Brookwood to Waterloo

Brookwood is the location of a multitude of famous graves. I have spent many hours walking its long, pleasant paths on sunny afternoons and observing its inhabitants. The renowned novelist Dennis Wheatley rests close to the main entrance. The celebrated author of such occult classics as The Devil Rides Out and The Haunting of Toby Jugg sees many fans visit his grave.

Another of Brookwoods more macabre residents is a man with a connection to my native Edinburgh. Esteemed anatomist Robert Knox provided incredible advancement in surgery throughout the early 1800s. Groups numbering 400 would attend his lectures within the confines of Edinburgh

Surgeons Hall.

The critical material providers for his studies were a local pair by the names of William Burke and William Hare. In November of 1828, evidence materialised that Burke and Hare were providing Doctor Knox with corpses that they had murdered. The term "Burking" would be used to describe their cruel methods.

Burke would be executed, and Hare would travel to England and vanish. Doctor Knox, however, would claim no knowledge of his involvement and, although acquitted, would face scrutiny for years. He would follow a jaded career path until his death in 1862, followed by his interment, where he rests today.

There are tales of paranormal activity within the confines of Brookwood Cemetery. The ghostly sound emanating from undisclosed tombs has been recorded over the years. The sound of sobbing women and children has been witnessed in the dead of night. Another story exists concerning the sighting of a ghostly signalman. Bearing similarities to the famous Dickens story, the tale, although interesting, is not much else known.

My first visit to Brookwood Cemetery happened in 2007 and entirely by mistake. While travelling back from London Waterloo in the late hours, I encountered a confusing incident. While attempting to change trains to Aldershot, I departed the train at the wrong station. I stepped off at Brookwood.

I stood there stranded on the dark and deserted platform of Brookwood Station. Slightly inebriated and unsure of the trains, I soon realised that the train I had departed was the last one of the night. The staff has long gone, and not a soul to be seen. I walked around for a short while. I ended up in the long, tiled tunnel to the Cemetery. Realising my predicament and not remotely about to walk through the Cemetery at midnight, I headed back to the platform. I was now not alone.

At the platform, end stood a solitary female figure. After a short while, I called out and asked if there was another train, but there was no answer. The figure stood still and in the shadow of the platform, slightly out of sight.

Suddenly I was drawn to the distant sound of a train. It was approaching and slowing down. As the welcoming light of the carriageway illuminated the platform and the door opened, I realised that the stand was again unoccupied. Where the figure went, I do not know. I was the only passenger on that last train to Alton. I checked the carriages to satisfy my curiosity, but nobody was there.

The whole time I stood on that dark platform in the confines of Brookwood Cemetery, one piece of nostalgia continuously entered my head.

They filmed the end of The Omen here.

Leaving the Woking train station, you are presented with an underpass. The exit leads to charming tree-lined streets and, eventually, Heathside Road. An attractive and large property exists about halfway along. It is here that a terrifying tale occurred.

Two sisters living within the property in 1904 would witness a terrifying series of events. The middle-aged sisters, whose names are unknown, would begin to hear noises from within their newly acquired house. Moaning, screeching and terrible murmuring terrorised the sisters for months on end. Empty rooms with locked doors would play host to the continuous disturbances within the property.

To avoid scandal and any source of embarrassment, the woman locked her sister in the house's attic. After a while, one of the sisters had enough and wished to report the disturbances to the relevant authorities. However, her older sibling bluntly refused. Her thoroughly traumatised sibling would remain incarcerated in the confines of the attic space until she died in 1936.

When common knowledge of her terrible confinement became public, what happened to her sister was not known. Much is, however, learned of what happened afterwards.

Property owners have documented demented screams and howls of insanity echoing from the upstairs building. The ghostly sounds of footsteps emanating from the stairwell have led many to flee the house and sell up. Whether the disturbances continue today is not known.

Heathside Road, the site of a terrifying event

After visiting the house in 2022, the building remains in good condition, maintained and currently occupied. The setting is unchanged, and the property is utterly recognisable from a vintage photograph I used to find its location.

Our final tale of haunted Woking dates back to 1932. One afternoon a retired vicar, The Reverend Thomas Outram, walked the extensive Oriental Road. He eventually would arrive at St Paul's Church, Maybury, to assist in the service of holy communion.

The day would pass as expected, and the church attendees would leave and do their business. It would later transpire that the same Reverend Marshall had died two hours previous at his home on nearby Oriental Road. Was the acting Reverend Wilson Carlisle accompanied by a ghost that day?

St Pauls Church, the site of a ghostly mass

Selborne, Bordon and Beyond

T he final trip I carried out in the haunted realms of Surrey and Hampshire occurred in the Autumn of 2022. I awoke that morning to storm clouds, torrential rain, and general dreadful conditions. My Hampshire sidekick Dan Hill was picking me up at 10 am for a full day of research for this book. I prayed that the weather would change or even let up for a bit, but by the look of things, the weather well and truly jinxed us. We carried on regardless and ventured forth towards our first location that day.

Upon entering the village of Crondall, the location appeared instantly familiar. It is an idyllic English village featuring all the trademarks accompanying its charming appearance. The rows of shops and traditional properties all looked familiar; it turned out that I had dined here some years earlier at the wonderful Hampshire Arms. However, I was informed of a disappointing lack of ghost stories that night, the culinary delights more than made up for it.

All Saints Church dates to the 9th Century. After extensive alterations and reconstruction, the church is in excellent condition today. A wide, cobbled path leads from Croft Lane and directly to the church entrance. Just around the corner and up a long and old-fashioned road sits a landmark Crondall property. It is here that a spirit has been sighted.

In the direction of All Saints Church

Peter Underwood recalls a person's account in a newspaper from the 1930s. The reader states seeing a ghost of a uniformed soldier sighted in the vicinity of Crondall Church.

'Last night, Wednesday 2 November, being a perfect moonlit night, a friend suggested we enjoy an hour's cycle ride, so we set off to Crondall. The time was 10.15 pm when we reached the church. We had left our cycles against the wall of the churchyard and were about to go up the lime avenue to the church when we noticed a misty object coming, it seemed to us, from a carriage drive opposite the wall. We stood perfectly still and waited to see what it was when, to our amazement, we saw it was a rider on horseback dressed in what looked like the armour of Cromwellian days. Whatever it was rode right through the churchyard wall, up the avenue, and disappeared, it seemed to us, into the church. We waited about half an hour, hoping it would return, but we did not see it again.'

Other supernatural stories exist from the vicinity of the church. Cromwellian troops have been sighted walking along Croft Lane, guided within an unearthly mist. The sound of unnatural footsteps on the roof combined with banging and knocks to the church door played havoc at a wedding that day. On another occasion, a wedding within the church grounds was so interrupted by supernatural visitors that a guest required medical attention from shock.

The path where a ghostly rider is sighted

Other haunted locations in Crondall include Ewshot House. A documented incident from the 1900s describes phantom noises, including banging from behind bricked walls. The noisy spirit was a source of constant annoyance to the occupiers.

In 1840, Itchells Manor witnessed paranormal activity. Blamed for a murder that once occurred in the building, many sleepless nights were created by banging. The cause of which could never be discovered.

A spectral woman in grey has been sighted on no less than three occasions at a Crondall cottage. The exact address could not be located that day. It is written that a pleasant atmosphere accompanied this entity, a lady in a simple grey dress with a white head covering, which appeared twice to a witness. In the mid-2000s, the sound of footsteps and the unexplained adjustment of electrical items were experienced in possibly the same property.

Dan Hill outside All Saints Church, Crondall

Not only have such ghostly sightings appeared in the village, but my personal favourite involves a ghostly herd of sheep. Never appearing, this phantom flock can be heard moving along the roads, the occasional 'Baaaaaaaa' betraying their position.

With the rain ceased and the clouds making way for sunshine, Dan and I moved on to our following location. Selborne is a mere 3.9 miles from neighbouring Alton. This charming village is the former home of esteemed naturalist Revd Gilbert White. Selborne's links to the pioneering birdwatcher ensure an array of visitors annually. Some of them have even seen his ghostly figure first-hand. The naturalist Gilbert White has popped up in many places in the village, despite dying in the 1700s. Monks have also been reported in the village - a priory once stood here, and though the building has long since gone, its former occupants are less reluctant to leave.

The most recent ghostly encounter in the village occurred on 15 October 2009 at 4 pm. Walking along this lane with his metal detector, a witness spotted a figure standing by a gate on a hill, silhouetted against the sky. The figure wore a strange hat and a coat which came almost to the ground. The witness looked away for a few seconds when the figure vanished, with no obvious exit route. When the witness approached the gate, he realised the area was covered in thick mud, and no tracks were visible.

Selborne, adjacent to Gilbert Whites House

After a hearty lunch in The Selborne Arms and a cheerful conversation with its owner ("There are no ghosts in here!"), we took to the country roads of Hampshire once more and drove to nearby Petersfield. The first location of this attractive market town was the one-time Green Dragon Public House. Dan recognised the building from years ago and recalled it when it used to be a pub. The property now serves as a youth work project yet still holds the features from its time as The Green Dragon.

The pub was known as The Sun Inn from 1828 until 1976, when it changed to The Green Dragon. It was back in 1957 when a strange chain of events would feature in a local newspaper. The article in The Hants and Sussex News reads as follows:

Under the headline 'A quiet "ghost" at the Sun Inn

"Customers in the public bar of the Sun Inn, Petersfield, looked up from their beer mugs and stared. One of several beer jugs on a shelf had begun to swing to and fro on its hook. The others were not moving.

"To the licensee, Christopher Hamilton, and his wife, this was just another incident which has led them over the past 18 months to believe there is a ghost in the inn.

"They have heard strange noises, like footsteps, coming along the corridor from the spare room at the top of the stairs. Mrs Hamilton is convinced that the ghost is a small child.

"Recently, she heard a noise at 2 am. 'I heard a noise like someone playing marbles on the spare room floor. IT WAS SECURELY FASTENED when I got to the door, and I was too scared to go in.

"' Never before in our whole lives have we experienced anything like this,' she and her husband agree. Mr Hamilton does not mind the ghost. 'It's a very quiet one, really,' he says.

"' As long as it does not come along and stick a cold, clammy hand on my neck in the middle of the night, I don't care.'

"Does he believe in ghosts? Mr Hamilton shrugs his shoulders and admits the noises are very distinct.

"A Scotsman – he came here with his wife and family about 18 months ago – he whispered about the habits of the being.

"'It generally happens about 8 pm or 8.30 pm. We hear footsteps like a lively child running along the corridor from the spare room at the top of the stairs.

"'Thinking the kids were out of bed, my wife has run upstairs to find them sound asleep – and you always know when a child is shamming – and the passage is empty.'

"The couple have not told their twin seven-year-old daughters that they believe the house is haunted.

"Roderick, aged 12, has heard the noises. Until one night, he used to sleep in the room from which most of the noises came. He woke up terrified at a loud banging on the wall, appearing to come from inside the room.

"Customers, like Mr E Mells, a Petersfield baker, and Mr K Marshall, have heard the noises and seen the beer jug swinging on the hook of its own accord."

An image of the property from its time as The Green Dragon

The former Green Dragon/Sun Inn today

Whether the paranormal events continued over the following decades is unknown. With the building now under a different guise and used for other purposes, it would be interesting to know if anybody has seen or heard of any activity in recent years.

The day's last visit took us to the former garrison town of Bordon. Much like Aldershot, Bordon played host to the British Army for many years. Now in the process of redevelopment, the town has drastically changed. The military presence may have moved on to Sandhurst, Deepcut and Hereford, yet one truly incredible story remains.

The junction between Forest Road and Hendon Road is a regular Hampshire location. The road remains busy at most times of day and night because it is a direct route to nearby Chase Hospital. In June 1999, two friends met with one of the greatest unexplained mysteries in Hampshire's history.

Forest Road in 2022

The men were driving from Chase Hospital on the way back to a parent's house. The property, although unknown, sat very close to its current position on Forest Road. As the car turned from Forest Road and traversed onto Hendon Road, the journey from then on should have taken two minutes. Upon arriving at the family home, the man's parents met them with grave concern. They had been missing for an hour and forty minutes. Although only a few decades ago, neither man owned a mobile phone, thus rendering contact impossible. The men were completely unaware of any delay or reason why anybody would have considered them delayed, let alone concerned about them missing. The events have to this day, never been explained.

We now jump forward to March 2001. A similar event came to the attention of the local constabulary; only this time, the witness was a single person walking home that day. Upon arriving home, a stunned and thoroughly irate family member informed the witness that they had been missing for more than three hours. The shocked man insisted that he had merely been gone for five minutes and literally round the corner. Once again, the corner he had travelled was between Forest Road and Hendon Road.

The Hendon Road Junction in 2022

Similar events which involve the possibility of reported timeslips have materialised over the years. One such event occurred in Bond Street in Liverpool in 1996. A 2001 report from the Liverpool Echo relays the strange events.

One Saturday in July 1996, Frank (an off-duty policeman) and his wife

Carol visited Liverpool to shop. At Central Station, the couple split up. Carol went to Dillons Bookshop in Bold Street to purchase a copy of Irvine Welsh's book, Trainspotting, and Frank went to a record store in Ranelagh Street to look for a CD.

About 20 minutes later, he walked up the incline near the Lyceum, which leads onto Bold Street, intending to meet up with his wife in the bookshop, when he noticed he had somehow entered a 'dead spot' of quietness. Frank crossed the road and saw that Dillons Bookshop was no longer there. In its place stood a store named 'Cripps' over its two entrances. The policeman was understandably confused.

He looked in the window of Cripps and saw no books on display but women's handbags and shoes. The policeman turned around and saw that the people on Bold Street were wearing clothes that would have been in vogue in the Forties and Fifties; the men wore trilbies and long overcoats, and the women wore scarves, berets, pillboxes, and cartwheel hats and most of the ladies also wore gloves.

Then the possibility that he had somehow walked into the Bold Street of 40-odd years ago dawned on the policeman. Frank sighted a girl of about 20, dressed in the clothes of a mid-1990s girl; hipsters and a lime-coloured sleeveless top. The bag she carried had Miss Selfridges on it, which reassured the policeman that he was still partly in 1996. He smiled at the girl as she walked past him and entered Cripps.

As Frank followed her, the whole interior of the building changed in a flash to the interior of Dillons Bookshop. The policeman was back in his own time. He grabbed the girl by the arm at the bookshop entrance and asked her: "Did you see that then?" She calmly said, "Yeah. I thought it was a new shop that had just opened. I was going in to look at the clothes, and now it's a bookshop."

The girl just chuckled, shook her head, and walked out again. When Frank told his wife about the incident, she said she had not noticed anything strange, but Frank was adamant that he had not hallucinated the episode.

The Hampshire Timeslip incident is indeed fascinating due to its recent proximity. On the day of our visit, Dan and I walked along the junction and drove past and towards the direction of the hospital. We took the time to investigate the intersection and attempt to sense anything unusual. However, on this occasion, we were met by only the returning bad weather from earlier on, and hence our journey to Selborne, Bordon and Beyond had now concluded.

Cheers Dan.

The Isle of Wight

I first visited the Isle of Wight some years ago. It is a unique Hampshire location serviced to the mainland by several ferries. Dating back to the pre-Bronze Age, the Island is steeped in incredible history. The oldest records that give a name for the Isle of Wight are from the Roman Empire. It was called Vectis or Vecta in Latin and Iktis or Ouiktis in Greek. Latin Vecta, Old English Wiht and Old Welsh form Gueid and Guith were recorded from the Anglo-Saxon period. The Domesday Book is called The Island Wit. The modern Welsh name is Ynys Wyth (ynys meaning Island). These are all variant forms of the same name, Celtic.

The Island is one of the most critical areas in Europe for dinosaur fossils. The eroding cliffs often reveal previously hidden remains, particularly along the Back of the Wight. Dinosaur bones and fossilised footprints can be seen in and on the rocks around the Island's beaches, especially at Yaverland and Compton Bay. As a result, the Island has been nicknamed "Dinosaur Island" and included in the area known as The Jurassic Coast.

The Isle of Wight features grand views across its downs and rural countryside. A drive around the isle's many regions will impress you with its extensive rustic beauty. Sandown, Yarmouth, and Cowes are just a few locations to impress me over the years. Tales of smugglers, battles and much more abound from this charming Hampshire location. However, the subject from the Isle of Wight hugely impressed me was its many, many ghosts.

The Ghost Island, The Isle of Wight

In recent years, The Isle of Wight has acquired the impressive title of 'Ghost Island', the world's most haunted Island, a hefty tag indeed, yet one that remains thoroughly deserved. The Island features an abundance of fascinating, historic and terrifying tales. In this chapter, I shall relay a selection of my favourite stories.

The former royal residence, Osborne House, rests in East Cowes. Constructed in 1845 and initially owned by Lady Isabella Blachford, the building was sold to Queen Victoria and Prince Albert. Victoria had spent two holidays on the Isle of Wight as a young girl when her mother, the Duchess of Kent, rented Norris Castle, the estate next door to Osborne. They wanted a home removed from the stresses of court life. They soon realised that the house was too small for their needs and decided, with advisors, to replace it with a new, larger residence.

Queen Victoria died at Osborne on 22 January 1901, with two generations of her family present. Although she adored Osborne and featured strict instructions that Osborne would remain in the family, her children did not share the attachment. Over the coming years, Osbourne House would

134

serve under various guises and was acquired in 1986 by National Heritage. However, Queen Victoria and many other residents have never left.

If you can visit Osborne House, take the guided tour. It is here that you will see the bed chamber of Queen Victoria. It is in this room that the former Queen drew her last breath. Evidence states that visitors to the bed chamber have witnessed a scent within its confines. The sweet smell resembles perfume akin to that worn by Queen Victoria. The building staff documents that the perfect time to encounter the aroma is in the late afternoon when the visitors depart for the day, and the building is quiet.

An aerial view of Osborne House

Queen Victoria is not the only restless spirit to grace the building's glorious confines. Sometime in the early 1990s, a cleaner named Richard met with a frightening experience. The local man had worked in Osborne House for some years. A sceptic, he states that members of staff were discouraged by management to discuss any connection to ghosts.

While cleaning the stairs, he states that he encountered a frightening entity. Something was standing directly behind him and genuinely scared him that day. Although Richard says that his time working at Osborne House was enjoyable, that day's incident changed his outlook on the supernatural.

A long-serving custodian of the property met with a ghostly encounter one day. After finishing for the day, the man prepared to return to his accommodation upstairs in the building. He had forgotten his jacket and returned to what is known as The Durbar Wing. Here on the stairs, he witnessed a short man, not solid and resembling a shadow. He had no hesitation that what he saw was a ghost.

Other spirits reported within Osborne House include a woman in a white ballgown. The spectral woman sighted floating along corridors has alarmed staff and visitors, yet she appears calm and serene when seen. The sight of a young Indian boy has also been reported. The spirit is connected to furniture from the Durbar Room, and his appearance has coincided with reupholstery from gold to red material.

Ventnor Botanic Gardens is another of my favourite Isle of Wights haunted locations. If you are fortunate enough to visit this fantastic location on a warm summer's day, you shall be treated to an array of beautiful plants, shrubs, and flowers. The coastal area of the Isle of Wight landmark is emphasised by the warm breeze and cliffs. When the botanic gardens close for the day and darkness begins to fall, the Ventnor location becomes a quite different place to visit.

Blocks 2, 3, & 4, Royal National Hospital, Ventnor, I.W.

An old image of Ventnor Hospital, now a botanic garden

Isle of Wight ghost tours has existed since 1994. Expert storyteller and Island historian Marc Tuckey host the venture. Having attended several of his thoroughly informative (and terrifying) walks, I recommend any reader to seek out his tours.

Ventnor Botanic Gardens was the one-time site of a substantial and historic hospital with a suitably haunted legacy. The Royal National Hospital, Ventnor, opened in 1869 for the treatment of chest diseases - tuberculosis.

It consisted of several 'cottages' for the patients with a chapel in the centre.

At that time, the main treatment for such diseases was fresh air and sunshine - two elements that the location at St Lawrence could provide.

With the development of antibiotics for the treatment of tuberculosis, the need for the hospital diminished, and the design and state of the buildings made them unsuitable for any other purpose.

The hospital closed in 1964 and was demolished in 1969, and the local council acquired the land.

The hospital, considerable in size, would take a substantial period to complete its deconstruction. During the time of the demolition, strange events would commence. Strange events along the way would frighten builders; it was as if the building were fighting back.

Only when demolition commenced in a particular area would events take a turn for the worse. The old operating theatre was the final part of the hospital to go. At least three vehicles would be damaged while attempting to pull down the ward. A demolition ball would be so severely damaged that the entire cab was crushed by falling masonry. A bulldozer snapped whilst trying to pull down a wall. The strangest event came when workers attempting to lay a power line below the surface had to dig up the line when the power failed to commence. The puzzled builders were left bemused at the sight of the newly laid power line, entirely severed in two.

Spectral figures were sighted throughout the demolition. An evil figure sighted in the doorway of the operating theatre caused workers to drop their sledgehammers and flee in fright. The apparition of a small girl would also appear in the operating theatre and be witnessed on many occasions while work was conducted.

Even today, the car park area and the remaining tunnel, which would connect the hospital to the site below, see paranormal activity. Head along to the Ghost Island walks with Marc and co; you never know who or what you may meet.

Also in the Ventnor area is the wonderful Buddle Inn. The hostelry dates to the 16th century and features incredible stories. A famous location for smugglers, The Buddle Inn featured many remnants from this time, including tunnels and original features still visible today. The sight of a spectral figure sighted walking from the fireplace and across the bar has been witnessed many times. The man appears in very old-fashioned clothing featuring a long jacket and hat. Due to the ghost's appearance, he is presumed to be a customs man continuing to apprehend smugglers in the infamous Inn.

A short distance away are two other haunted locations. The Enchanted Manor is a hotel which dates to 1838. Previously known as Windcliffe Manor, the residence, sometimes referred to as "A romantic bolthole", has been successful with visitors to the Island for many years. The building features its ghost who, although an excellent addition to the location, has scared visitors to its realms.

A short walk down a steep hill offers the visitor incredible coastal views across The English Channel. Upon the descent, two large stone pillars greet you and signal the halfway marker. Upon reaching the bottom of the steep gravel path, you are confronted by the sight of the magnificent St Catherine's Lighthouse. The lighthouse, operated by Trinity House, is now holiday cottages.

The first lighthouse was established on St Catherine's Down in 1323 on the orders of the Pope after a ship ran aground nearby and its cargo was either lost or plundered. Once it was part of St Catherine's Oratory, its octagonal stone tower can still be seen on the hill west of Niton. The new lighthouse, built by Trinity House in 1838, was constructed as a 40-metre stone tower. Its height would be reduced for operational difficulties when obscured by thick coastal fog.

A visit to haunted St Catherine's Lighthouse

As with any site of historical tragedy, St. Catherine's Lighthouse has its fair share of ghost sightings. Visitors have reported seeing the spirits of the lighthouse keepers killed during the air raid walking the grounds, performing their duties as if the attack never occurred. Others have reported objects inside the lighthouse moving independently and sometimes disappearing entirely. Curiously, there are also numerous reports of ghost animals on the premises, though it is unknown why this might be the case. The ghost of a former lighthouse keeper's beloved dog?

It is no surprise that visitors to St. Catherine's Lighthouse keep an eye out for paranormal activity. The area surrounding the lighthouse, while beautiful, feels remote and otherworldly. And since the lighthouse engaged in the recent tragedy, it is hard to visit without thinking of the lighthouse keepers that met their tragic end and all the lives lost at sea.

You have arrived at the legendary Knighton Gorges, once the grandest building on The Isle of Wight and most certainly the most haunted. I have visited Knighton Gorges on several occasions. The sight of the roaming downs is pleasant, and the thick, leafy copses are impressive yet challenging to even the most experienced motorists. As you descend the densely covered Knighton Shute and eventually glimpse the imposing stone pillars, you are met with a sense of something special.

None of the Isle of Wight's haunted locations can match the fascinating tale of Knighton Gorges.

The grand manor estate of Knighton Gorges is documented as constructed in the 12th century. It was titled 'The Grandest Building on the Island' and encapsulated various stories.

One of the earliest owners of Knighton was said to be Hugh de Morville, who, on the night of 29 December 1170, was one of four knights who murdered Thomas Becket at Canterbury Cathedral.

Hugh returned to Knighton after the assassination and believed the house to be cursed, through a projection of his guilt. Hugh then fled to Knaresborough Castle in North Yorkshire, and the house remained in his family until it was passed onto Ralf de Gorges, who acquired the property via marriage in 1256. At this time, 'Gorges' was added onto the property's name 'Knighton'.

A few hundred years later, in 1565, Antony Dillington bought Knighton from Thomas Gilbert and began necessary renovations on the old home. Antony incorporated some rooms from the original building into the new house as part of the restoration process, including a room with the inscription 'The Room of Tears' engraved over the door.

While the house still stood, some witnesses claimed the occasional, unexplained sound of sweet music haunted the Room of Tears. It is said that a former owner named Sir Theobald Russell died in the room from wounds sustained from battle. Shortly after his death, Theobald's wife, Lady Gorges, passed in the room from a broken heart.

The legendary Knighton Gorges

A slightly more morbid piece of Knighton Gorges's history involves Tristram Dillington's death by self-inflicted gunshot on 7 July 1721 at 41. He was driven to despair after losing his wife and all but one of his children, from smallpox. Other sources say an incredible debt was involved after Dillington turned to gamble as a coping mechanism.

Since suicide was considered a sin, a law at the time would have forced all Dillington's assets to be handed over to the Crown, including Knighton Gorges. To stop this from occurring, Dillington's steward stepped up to ensure the manor stayed in the Dillington family. To make Dillington's death appear an accident instead of a suicide, the steward strapped the deceased's body to his favourite horse Thunderbolt and forced the horse to run into the pond below the manor. The steward then relayed that Dillington, who often rode his horse home at night, lost his way in the darkness and drowned after running into the pond. How the steward explained, the shotgun wound is uncertain, but his story was believable enough that Knighton Gorges was passed down to Dillington's sisters, Hannah, and Mary.

However, there are rumours that despite Dillington's death surpassing suspicion of the law, he was not given a Christian burial. A stone in a church in Newchurch displays his name along with his family's, but it is said that Dillington is not buried there. The story goes that the skeleton of a large man was found buried in the Knighton Gorges walled garden, and it is thought that this was Dillington's actual resting place.

The ghost stories connected with Knighton Gorges and its surrounding area are incredible.

Between 1927 and 1977, there have been half a dozen recorded sightings of a ghost in the grounds. The apparition is that of Tristram Dillington and is sighted on 7 July, the date of his death. The terrifying spectral figure was sighted riding a horse and carriage throughout the grounds of Knighton Gorges.

The imposing construction is all that remains of Knighton Gorges today. Many visitors to Knighton Gorges stop and observe the great stone pillars at the entrance. Visitors have described a host of decorative stone statues on the top of the posts for many years. However, nothing remains and has for a long time. Gargoyles, dogs, and other objects have all been described by members of the public. On one occasion, an Island resident named Edwin Perry wrote to a local newspaper complaining that the decorative centre piece had been stolen. Did it ever exist at all?

The pillars of haunted Knighton Gorges

To many revellers, visitors to the Island and those interested in the paranormal, New Year is the time to visit.

For many years witnesses have reported apparitions within the area of Knighton Gorges sighted on New Year's Eve.

In local folklore, it is said that a peddler travelling along the nearby Knighton Shute came across an unusual sight on New Year's Eve. The man searching for food and a place to rest witnessed a large manor house with lights on that frosty winter night. Bypassing the large concrete pillars, he walked the steep path to the large manor house. To his joy, the man soon realised that a party was in full swing. The New Year's celebrations echoed from the property, so he entered.

The peddler claims that after eating and drinking with fellow revellers, he left the party and ventured upon his merry way. The party had been a joyous event, and he not only enjoyed fellow attendees' company but also danced and conversed with them that night.

After relaying the story to a resident, the man's revelations were put down to drunkenness and sheer nonsense. The resident informed the stunned traveller that there was no such building near Knighton Gorges and had not existed for many years.

Who did the bewildered man dance, drink, and chat with that frosty night? Could it have been another instance of the restless ghosts of Knighton Gorges?

Power loss to vehicles around Knighton Shute is nothing new. A story from 1985 states that a resident of the Island named Mark Fisher had difficulty in the autumn of that year. Mark, out for a run on his motorbike, decided that evening to take a run past the site of Knighton Gorges. Mark panicked when he approached the stone pillars as his 125cc bike packed in, and the power ceased. The power failure resulted in the enraged man pushing his bike up the steep road towards his home.

The following day Mark visited a garage where the mechanic deemed nothing wrong with his vehicle. It was at this point that garage staff relayed ghostly tales of the location where his bike had broken down. Mark, having only lived on the Island for a year, was stunned by the revelations of the laughing mechanic. He states that he has since passed the area many times but has only had a powerful, more significant, and more reliable motorcycle since the incident.

Legendary Isle of Wight author Gay Baldwin encountered strange phenomena while filming for the first IOW Ghost Island video in 1994. While filming at Knighton Gorges, a series of bizarre events plagued the production. Repetitive interference from cars, motorbikes and many other obstacles would cease filming every time the crew commenced recording.

A woodcut of Knighton Gorges

I have encountered similar technical oddities on a few occasions while filming for North Edinburgh Nightmares projects. The first instance involved filming a section on the grounds of the world-famous Greyfriars Cemetery in late August one year. Each time we attempted recording, the sound would appear distorted and unusable. North Edinburgh Nightmares collaborator Kerrie remembers that on that afternoon, not only was the sound mysteriously distorted, the grave in which she filmed before became infested and swarmed in an unnatural mass of crawling ladybirds. It was the only grave in the large cemetery affected in such a way, but it continued each time we commenced filming.

On my first trip to the Island, I spotted a leaflet while out in the charming village of Godshill. The A5 flyer proudly proclaimed the title 'Ghost Island' across its suitably spooky design. The advert was my introduction to the fantastic ghost walks of Mark Tuckey. That evening I ventured to Newport on the long-running Wednesday night Ghost Walk. A host of fascinating and terrifying stories would follow that pleasant summer evening; we were treated to the most chilling one.

The Castle Inn, situated at 91 High Street, is the oldest pub in Newport. Dating back to 1550, the pub remains suitably traditional and presents many original features. Previously used as a venue for cock fighting, The Castle Inn was once the haunt of ruffians, villains, and smugglers. The pub has seen many proprietors over the years and has seen its difficulties in the bargain.

The Castle Inn, Newport, Isle of Wight

There have been reports of an apparition that enjoys switching on the television at night. Sometimes, the spirit wants a selection of music into the bargain (rock music appears to be the genre of choice). The one ghost that seems to have never gone away is that of a stable boy. Presumed hanged in the now function suite, it is unknown if he did so by suicide, due to debt. The tragic figure was witnessed in the room at the rear of the building. Paranormal groups and psychics have attempted to contact him on several occasions, with extraordinary evidence being recorded. The spirit enjoys moving five-pence pieces throughout the pub. Witnesses have described discovering small piles of coins in the windows and corners of the Inn when visiting.

The last time I visited The Castle Inn was on 5 September 2019. Upon entering the Inn, I noticed that the pub was under new management and quiet that afternoon. A calm and relaxed afternoon would ensue. I spoke to bar staff about the pub's history; sadly, they were new and had no ghostly tales for me on this occasion. I attempted to place a small pile of coins on the window recess where I sat and, at the end of my visit, checked to see if they had been moved. Unfortunately, there was nothing at all.

The barn of The Castle Inn

Before leaving, I visited the toilet and sporadically remembered the story of the barn. The large function hall sits at the rear of the pub. Old wooden beams decorate the ceiling, and the location has a genuine old-fashioned feel. It reminds me of an ancient bowling alley from the confines of Edinburgh's famous Sheep Heid pub. I was out of the door and about to leave when I heard a knock from the room's rear. It was only the slightest of noise, yet enough to alert me to the sound. There was nobody there whatsoever. The incident left a genuine chill and a feeling that I was undoubtedly being watched.

Many stories from The Isle of Wight are ghostly and suitably frightening. Quarr Abbey, The Buddle Inn and The Castle Hotel in Ryde are some of my favourites, and I recommend visiting them all. The Island has an atmosphere all its own. I always remember the ferry from Portsmouth as it docks at Fishbourne, and another haunted adventure commences. I shall certainly return someday soon and continue to discover the legendary, chilling, exciting, historical ghosts of The Isle of Wight.

A place I shall never forget.

Bibliography

The Haunted Places of Hampshire, Ian Fox

Haunted Inns of Hampshire, Roger Long

Haunted Hampshire, Anthony Brody

The Original Ghosts of The Isle of Wight, Gay Baldwin

More Ghosts of The Isle of Wight, Gay Baldwin

Ghosts of The Isle of Wight Three, Gay Baldwin

Isle of Wight Ghosts Book Four, Gay Baldwin

Even More Ghosts, Gay Baldwin

Ghost Island Book Five, Gay Baldwin

Most Haunted Island Book Six, Gay Baldwin

Ghosts of Knighton Gorges, Gay Baldwin

Haunted Places of Surrey, John Janaway

Ghosts of Surrey, John Janaway

Haunted Farnham, Peter Underwood

Ghosts of Hampshire and The Isle of Wight, Peter Underwood

Haunted Guildford, Philip Huthinson

Paranormal Surrey, Rupert Matthews

Haunted Hampshire, Rupert Matthews

The Liverpool Echo

The Petersfield Post

The Darkside Magazine

Fortean Times

About the Author

John Tantalon has been interested in Edinburgh's folklore and ghost stories for many years. His first book 'North Edinburgh Nightmares' (2020), covers many lesser-known tales from the city. The anthology of sixteen ghostly tales would provide the blueprint for a sequel the following year.

John would produce a series of short films to accompany the stories from the books. The stories have proved a great success and continue to thrill viewers today. The North Edinburgh Nightmares you-tube channel features 28 separate short films.

You can connect with me on:
- https://northedinburghnightmares.wordpress.com
- https://twitter.com/NightmaresNorth?ref_src=twsrc%5Egoogle%7Ctwcamp%5Eserp%7Ctwgr%5Eauthor
- https://www.facebook.com/john.tantalon
- https://linktr.ee/johntantalon

Also by John Tantalon

North Edinburgh Nightmares

The City of Edinburgh, also known as Auld Reekie is a city steeped in history. A location saturated in ghostly tales, a macabre legacy and a catalogue of things that go bump in the night. In this anthology, I present to you sixteen stories you may never have encountered before.The North of Edinburgh conveys a rich and varied past. Castles, stately homes, harbours and dockland are just some of the locations to feature in the pages of this book, each with a terrifying story to tell. Could a cursed ornament unleash a reign of terror over a small seaside town and leave without a trace?What lies at the bottom of the mysterious Wardie Steps that has terrified so many travellers over the years?What caused a night security guard to flee a 500-year-old castle in the Blackhall area of the city in the dead of night, not once but on three separate occasions? Could a long-forgotten Leith landmark hold the answer to evil activity in its vicinity?These and many more terrifying tales lie within.North Edinburgh Nightmares

Beyond North Edinburgh Nightmares

Welcome to Beyond North Edinburgh Nightmares.

Edinburgh and its Burghs provide the backdrop for this sequel to my previous book
(North Edinburgh Nightmares).

Over the last year, I have ventured to many different locations and interviewed residents of the areas. People from all over the city and beyond recall their ghostly encounters, mysterious incidents and tales that go bump in the night.

Printed in Great Britain
by Amazon